CONTEMPORARY SOCIAL RESEARCH SERIES
General Editor: MARTIN BULMER

2

Modelling Society

CONTEMPORARY SOCIAL RESEARCH SERIES

Modelling Society

An Introduction to Loglinear Analysis for Social Researchers

G. NIGEL GILBERT
University of Surrey

London
GEORGE ALLEN & UNWIN
Boston   Sydney

George Allen & Unwin (Publishers) Ltd,
40 Museum Street, London WC1A 1LU, UK

George Allen & Unwin (Publishers) Ltd,
Park Lane, Hemel Hempstead, Herts HP2 4TE, UK

Allen & Unwin Inc.,
9 Winchester Terrace, Winchester, Mass 01890, USA

George Allen & Unwin Australia Pty Ltd,
8 Napier Street, North Sydney, NSW 2060, Australia

First published in 1981

British Library Cataloguing in Publication Data

Gilbert, G. Nigel
  Modelling society. – (Contemporary social research
series; 2)
1. Log–linear models   2. Social sciences–Statistical
methods
I. Title   II. Series
519.5   QA278
ISBN 0–04–312009–1
ISBN 0–04–312010–5 pbk

Library of Congress Cataloging in Publication Data

Gilbert, G. Nigel.
  Modelling society.
(Contemporary social research series; 2)
Bibliography: p.
Includes index.
1. Social surveys–Methodology.   2. Log–linear models.
I. Title.   II. Series.
HN29.G5   300'.7'2   81–10976
ISBN 0–04–312009–1   AACR2
ISBN 0–04–312010–5 (pbk.)

Set in 11 on 12 point Times by Computacomp (UK) Ltd, Fort William,
Scotland
and printed in Great Britain
by Biddles Ltd, Guildford, Surrey

Contents

Editor's Preface

The structure of the social sciences combines two separate elements, theory and empirical evidence. Both are necessary for successful social understanding; one without the other is barren. The *Contemporary Social Research* series is concerned with the means by which this structure is maintained and kept standing solid and upright, a job performed by the methodology of social research.

The series is intended to provide concise introductions to significant methodological topics. Broadly conceived, research methodology deals with the general grounds for the validity of social scientific propositions. How do we know what we do know about the social world? More narrowly, it deals with the questions 'how do we actually acquire new knowledge about the world in which we live?', 'what are the strategies and techniques by means of which social science data are collected and analysed?' The series will seek to answer such questions through the examination of specific areas of methodology.

Why is such a series necessary? There exist many solid, indeed massive, methodology textbooks, with which most undergraduates in sociology, psychology and the other social sciences acquire familiarity in the course of their studies. The aim of this series is different. It goes beyond such texts to focus upon specific topics, procedures, methods of analysis and methodological problems to provide readable introductions to its subjects. Each book contains annotated suggestions for further reading. The intended audience includes the advanced undergraduate, the graduate student, the working social researcher seeking to familiarise himself with new areas, and the non-specialist who wishes to enlarge his knowledge of social research. Research methodology need not be remote and inaccessible. Some prior knowledge of statistics will be useful, but only certain titles in the series will make strong statistical demands upon the reader. The series is concerned above all to demonstrate the general importance and centrality of research methodology to social science.

Nigel Gilbert's *Modelling Society* provides a lucid and straightforward introduction to an important new type of quantitative data analysis. Developed gradually over the last fifteen years, the procedure is associated particularly with the name of Leo

Goodman, Professor of Sociology and Statistics at the University of Chicago. The available literature up to the present time on the subject has been highly mathematical and statistical, rendering these significant developments rather inaccessible to social scientists who do not have a strong background in mathematics. Nigel Gilbert presents the ideas and procedures of loglinear analysis in an intelligible and non-mathematical manner, based on his experience of teaching social science graduate students. Additional advice is provided on computing procedures. The book will commend itself as a valuable and relatively non-technical introduction.

MARTIN BULMER
*The London School of Economics
and Political Science*

Author's Preface

The results of social surveys usually include classifications, cross-tabulations and often attitude and preference scales. These are the kinds of quantitative data that many social researchers have to deal with. Yet most researchers are taught methods of data analysis – regression, analysis of variance and factor analysis, for example – which were mainly developed in the biological sciences to deal with quite different kinds of measurements. One consequence of this is that many researchers do not realise how much could be learnt from their data by using more appropriate methods. More dangerously, some have applied the methods they know regardless of the form of their data, risking spurious or meaningless results. This book provides an introduction to a new technique, loglinear analysis, which is specifically intended to get the most out of categorical data, the kind of data which social researchers probably encounter most often. Loglinear analysis has been developed into a useful tool only during the last decade (the major contributions were made by Goodman, 1964–79; Haberman, 1974; and Bishop, Fienberg and Holland, 1975). Because it is relatively new, almost all the literature describing loglinear analysis is directed at the professional statistician and not at the practising researcher. This book is intended to fill that gap, presenting an informal description of the technique, illustrated with numerous examples from social research.

As an introduction, it will be of interest to undergraduate and postgraduate sociology students, but it contains much that is also likely to be unfamiliar to many practising researchers including not only academic sociologists, but also the rapidly growing band of professionals who use the tools of social research in diverse applied contexts, such as education, health, the social services and planning. The discussion should be easily understandable to anyone with a knowledge of basic statistics and some acquaintance with simple regression.

Although this is an introductory guide and so cannot include every detail, the reader should be able to tackle a loglinear analysis on the basis of what is in the book. Since the technique is impossibly tedious without the assistance of a computer, no details of computational methods have been included, but the final chapter lists some computer programs which can perform the necessary calculations. Most academic institutions already have one or more of these programs installed on their computers.

Numerous people have been involved in the preparation of this book. Whilst it was being written, I tried out portions of it on unsuspecting generations of students following the University of Surrey's M.Sc. course in social research. Peter Abell, Sara Arber, Martin Bulmer, George Brown, Keith Macdonald, Ken Prandy, Mike Procter and Asher Tropp read drafts and were kind and helpful with their comments. I am also indebted to a computer – the PRIME system at the University of Surrey – for help in computation and for the text-processing system on which the major part of the book was composed.

G. NIGEL GILBERT
Department of Sociology,
University of Surrey

1

Real and Imaginary Worlds

Table 1.1 shows some data derived from a survey of a community in Oldham. People were asked whether they themselves owned or rented their homes, and whether their parents had owned or rented theirs. You will see that some areas of the table are filled with zeros. The numbers in the rows and columns concerned with owner-occupiers are on the whole larger than the rest. These are two obvious instances of the patterns which can be found in a data table; ones which can be found from a simple visual inspection. But there may be many other, more complex patterns in this data which are not so easy to see. Detecting these calls for more sophisticated methods, involving the use of statistical techniques.

Researchers are interested in such patterns, because they provide clues to the underlying social processes which generated the data. If we want to understand those social processes, we need to be able to analyse their manifestations in the data we collect. For instance, we might suppose that the present form of housing tenure of the Oldham respondents is influenced to some degree by whether their parents owned or rented their houses. This seems a likely possibility given the fact that many other aspects of people's life style are inherited. If there is indeed a tendency for parents' tenure to influence sons' and daughters' tenure, then this ought to be reflected in the pattern of numbers in Table 1.1. Specifically, the entries along the top left to bottom right diagonal ought to be larger than one would otherwise expect. In later chapters, we shall see how one can calculate the entries one would otherwise expect, and so discover whether there is an intergenerational inheritance of tenure.

One way to examine tables such as this one is to look for all the patterns which can be found in it. There is something to be said for such an approach as a starting-point, especially if one is rather ignorant about the social processes which might have generated the

Table 1.1   *Intergenerational Change in Housing Tenure*

| | | *Respondent's present form of tenure* | | | | | |
	Owner-occupied	*Rented from local council*	*Unfurnished, rented from private landlord*	*Furnished, rented from private landlord*	*Other*	*Don't know. question not asked*	*Total*
Parents' tenure							
Owner-occupied	84	2	7	12	0	0	105
Rented from council	39	3	2	1	1	1	47
Unfurnished, privately rented	77	5	13	0	3	0	98
Furnished, privately rented	4	0	2	0	0	0	6
Other	18	1	1	0	0	0	20
Don't know, not asked	117	2	26	4	1	0	150
Total	339	13	51	17	5	1	426

Source: derived from Crosby, 1978, table 21.

data. However, there are almost always a large number of patterns to be found in *any* data table, if one looks hard enough. Some of these will be interesting and true reflections of the processes we wish to investigate. Others will be spurious, appearing quite by chance and reflecting nothing in particular. An analogy might be helpful to illustrate how such spurious patterns could arise. The Ancients looked for patterns amongst the stars in the night sky and found the signs of the Zodiac – stars which to them appeared to be arranged to form the outlines of the Zodiac symbols: a ram, a crab, a lion, and so on. We know now that although there is some patterning in the night sky (the Milky Way is, for instance, the most visible indication of the galaxy in which we live), the Zodiac pattern is spurious, reflecting no real structures in the universe. In much the same way, we can always find some pattern in research data, but finding it does not establish that the pattern is of any theoretical or substantive significance.

A better approach to examining data is to draw on one's prior theoretical knowledge and insight about the social processes which might be involved, and to test whether the data shows the consequences of those processes. In other words, we use a theoretical *model* of what we think might be happening to guide the search for patterns in the data. A model is a theory or set of hypotheses which attempts to explain the connections and inter-relationships between social phenomena. Models are made up of concepts and relationships between concepts.

The idea of a model can be illustrated with an example involving a very simple relationship. Suppose that we are studying the effect of education on social status. Education and social status are the two concepts we are concerned with. Theoretical ideas would suggest that, other things being equal, the higher one's educational attainment, the higher is one's status. Our very straightforward model is, then, that 'status and education are directly related'. One would have confidence in the validity of this model, if data on education and status were obtained and it was found that the two were, indeed, directly related. In practice, however, one cannot easily measure 'education' and 'status'. Instead one would have to resort to using *indicators* of the concepts. Possibly adequate but crude indicators in this instance might be 'the number of years at school or other educational establishments' (to measure education), and 'the rating of current occupation on a scale of occupational prestige' (to measure status). If we collected data using these indicators and if we found that this data showed a direct relationship between the two, this could be taken as evidence that the model is correct. We would have found a *structural correspondence* between the relationship posited in the model and the relationship discovered in the data. Figure 1.1 illustrates the connections between actual

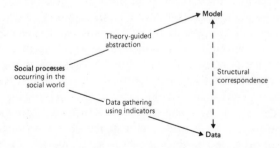

Figure 1.1   *The relationship between a model and data.*

social processes, a model and the data one obtains from indicators.

Let's suppose that we have found such a structural correspondence. What does this tell us? It suggests that the relationship specified in the model may exist in the 'real world' or, to put it another way, that the model can represent that portion of the 'real world' we have studied. The model can be used to make predictions about how the 'real world' will respond to changes. Moreover, the relationships specified in the model will also serve as an explanation of how the 'real world' works.

Nevertheless, one must be rather cautious about jumping to the conclusion that a model is a correct representation of the 'real world' from the discovery of structural correspondence alone. Such correspondence only provides evidence in support of the model, not definite confirmation of its validity. This is because the chain of argument leading to a demonstration of correspondence is a long and fairly complicated one, involving the derivation of a model from theory, the choice of indicators appropriate for testing the model, the collection of data using those indicators and, finally, a decision on whether correspondence has or has not been found. There is room for error in each of these steps.

Moreover, even if a model is correct, it never provides the full story. Inevitably, all models are simplified representations of the 'real world'. Not every pertinent relationship that exists can be included in the model. For instance, educational attainment is certainly not the only determinant of status, nor is it even the most important. An enormous range of other factors influences one's status. A model can, therefore, only serve to provide a partial explanation and can only give an imperfect guide to prediction. This is of course especially true of a model as simple as the education and status example above, but it is also the case with the considerably more complicated models we shall meet in later chapters.

With these general ideas in mind, let us now look more closely at how one establishes whether there is 'structural correspondence' between models and data. Once a suitable model has been formulated by a researcher, he could be said to locate it in an 'imaginary world'. This is identical in all respects to the 'real world', *except* that the 'imaginary world' includes the relationships specified in the model. Thus, the 'imaginary world' is the world which would exist if the model were true. For instance, to return to the earlier example, in order to test the education/status model, one creates in imagination a world identical to our own, except that in *this* world education is directly related to status.

Now one can compare the 'imaginary world' with the 'real world'. If the two are indistinguishable, that is evidence for concluding that the model is correct. If the 'imaginary world', which incorporates the model relationships, differs from the 'real world' (in which the relationships are the real but unknown ones), this is evidence that the model is incorrect. The problem of establishing structural correspondence is, therefore, reduced to the problem of comparing the 'real' and the 'imaginary' worlds. The comparison is performed by making measurements in both worlds. Data from the 'real world' is obtained by observation, questionnaires and the other usual collection procedures. Data from the 'imaginary world' is obtained, using one of the data analysis techniques – regression, factor analysis, loglinear analysis, multidimensional scaling, or whatever is appropriate. These techniques generate the data (often called *expected* or *fitted* data) which one would have expected to collect, if the 'imaginary world' had really existed.

Thus we obtain two data sets, one from the real observation of the 'real world' and one from the analytic technique which has been used to simulate the collection of data from the 'imaginary world'. If the two sets of data are identical, or are at least sufficiently nearly identical, this provides evidence for supposing that the 'real' and 'imaginary' worlds are in fact the same; or in short, that the model may correctly represent the true state of affairs. The connections between these worlds is illustrated in Figure 1.2.

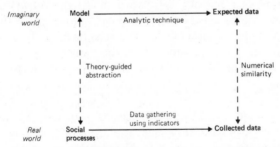

Figure 1.2 *Schematic diagram, illustrating the relationship between the 'real' and 'imaginary' worlds.*

At this point, we can set out the steps one needs to perform in order to analyse a set of data:

(1) From prior theoretical knowledge and the investigator's own insights, a model is designed to encapsulate the relationships thought to be important in the problem area to be studied.

(2) A choice is made about the analytical technique to be used. This will be determined both by the form of the model to be examined, and by the type of data which can be obtained.

(3) The model is restated in terms appropriate to the analytic technique to be used.

(4) The model and analytic technique are used in combination to generate a set of 'expected' data (the data from the 'imaginary world').

(5) The 'expected' data is compared with the data actually collected.

(6) A decision is made about whether the model is acceptable, depending on whether the 'expected' and 'observed' data sets are sufficiently similar.

(7) If the two data sets are not sufficiently similar, the model is rejected and steps 1–7 are repeated with another model, designed taking note of the differences found between the data sets.

(8) If the model does appear to be acceptable, it is examined to see whether it can be simplified and refined. As in science generally, a simpler explanation is preferable to an unnecessarily complex one. The process of refinement will involve testing the acceptability of simpler models, following steps 1–8.

(9) Before carrying out step 9, we shall only know that certain relationships exist, but it is also useful to discover the relative importance or strength of these relationships. This is done by calculating the 'parameters' of the model.

(10) Thus, we arrive at a model which is adequate for our own data.

To validate the model, it is necessary to test it on another independent set of data. However, one does not often have a second set of data available, and so it is rarely practical for the analyst to perform a validation. More usually, other researchers play the major role in validating models. Sometimes this may take the form of a strict replication of the analysis on other data. Much more frequently, the model which has been developed to explain data taken from one context is 'tested' on data derived from different but related contexts. Flesh will be put on the bones of this scheme in the following chapters, in which there are numerous examples of how it works in practice.

The scheme outlined above differs in two main ways from the 'classical' approach to data analysis. First, statistical texts, especially ones pitched at an elementary level, generally consider the testing of 'hypotheses' rather than models. The term 'model' has been used here partly because it seems clearer than 'hypothesis', and partly because whilst a hypothesis usually concerns just one relationship, a model may and usually does involve a complex set of linked relationships. Secondly, the 'classical' approach assumes that the analyst possesses, *a priori*, a carefully formulated hypothesis to be tested with the data. Following the confirmation or rejection of this hypothesis, the analyst must cease working with the original set of data. Further, improved hypotheses must be tested with new data. In contrast, the above scheme assumes that, whilst the analyst should have some prior theoretical notions about the form of suitable models, the investigation ceases only when an adequate model to describe the one set of data has been found. The task is essentially to *explore* in depth the structure of the data. This seems a much more realistic view of the role of the analyst than the classical one, and it is an approach which is increasingly being adopted by statisticians under the name of *exploratory data analysis* (Tukey, 1977).

Summary

Exploratory data analysis seeks to construct and test models against data collected from the social world. The models are intended to account for theoretically significant patterns in the data. In order to assess the validity of a model, an analytic technique is used to generate expected data, the data which would have been obtained if the model did correctly represent the real world, and this data and the observed data are compared. The essence of the exploratory approach to analysis is that successive models are examined to find the one which best fits the data.

Further Reading

The relationship between theory and data is one which has exercised sociologists and philosophers of science for many years. The view outlined in this chapter is developed more extensively in Willer

(1967); Blalock (1971) considers the 'gap' between theory and data from another angle. Abell (1971) advocates a 'model-building perspective' and discusses the components of such models: concepts, variables, propositions and relations, in a careful but readable way. Tukey's techniques for exploratory data analysis are applied to social research in Erickson and Nosanchuk (1977).

2

Classification and Measurement

Quantitative data may be collected in a host of different ways, but common to all is the process of classification. For instance, we may want to count the number of events, people, or actions occurring in a particular social setting. But before we can do the counting, we must classify what is to be counted: thus, to find out how many children there are in a school, we need first to classify those in the school into 'children' and 'others' (teachers, secretaries, cleaners, and so on).

Although classification may seem an uncomplicated task, a great deal comes to depend on just how it is done. If the right categories are not chosen at the start, no amount of statistical analysis will come to the rescue. There are four main aspects of classification which need attention: the categories must all relate to some common property; the items to be classified into a category must be sufficiently similar with respect to that common property for them to be considered identical for analytical purposes; the categories must be mutually exclusive; and the set of categories must be exhaustive. Let us consider each of these in turn.

The categories we choose for a classification must all be concerned with the same idea. It would not be sensible to ask 'are you male or aged over 21?' as an item on a questionnaire, and thus categorise people into two groups, the 'males' and the 'over 21s'. The question and the categories it suggests are based on two quite different variables: sex and age. To categorise the information we need two questions, one about sex and one about age, and two separate classifications. Putting it more formally, we might say that a classification should be based on one, and only one, *property* of the items being classified.

It is not always so obvious that a set of categories relates to more than one property. Consider the categories listed in Table 2.1, which

Table 2.1   *Question on Ethnic Affiliation*

10(1)	Race or ethnic group			
	Please tick the appropriate box	1	| |	White
	to show the race or ethnic group	2	| |	West Indian
	to which the person belongs or from	3	| |	African
	which the person is descended	4	| |	Arab
		5	| |	Chinese
		6	| |	Indian
		7	| |	Pakistani
		8	| |	Bangladeshi
		9	| |	Sri Lankan

If Indian, Pakistani, Bangladeshi or
Sri Lankan, please also tick one box
below

Hindu	Sikh	Muslim	Other
| |	| |	| |	| |
12	13	14	15

Source: adapted from OPCS, 1978 p. 6.

shows part of an early version of a question designed by the Office of Population Censuses and Surveys (OPCS) to measure ethnic affiliation. Inspection shows that the list of 'ethnic groups' seems to consist of a muddle of categories based on racial (for example, white), geographical (African), religious (Hindu) and cultural (Arab) characteristics (Mack, 1978). Interpreted strictly, one's ethnic affiliation depends on one's culture, and the other properties, race, geography and religion, should have no part in a classification of ethnicity. The confusion which results from having categories relating to a number of properties in one classification was noted and OPCS subsequently prepared improved versions of this question.

A second highly desirable feature of a classification is that each category should include only items which are the same or very similar on the property being measured. For instance, until the 1971 Census the Registrar-General classified occupations into five 'classes', from I, which included 'professional' occupations, to V, the 'unskilled' occupations. But class III in the original scheme covered all skilled jobs, both manual and non-manual. The great diversity of occupations in class III meant that there was little one could say in general about them. Recognising this problem, since 1971 OPCS has subdivided class III into a non-manual and a manual component (OPCS, 1970). Each of the new categories includes a much more homogeneous group of occupations than the original large class.

Thirdly, the categories in a classification must be mutually exclusive; that is, all the items to be classified must find a place in only one of the categories. If one is classifying using numbers, for instance, by age, all that need be remembered is that the category boundaries must not overlap. It is easy when drafting a questionnaire to fall into the trap of categorising age into the ranges: 16–25, 25–45, etc.; but this is a mistake, for those aged 25 can be placed in either the first or second category. The ranges must be altered to make them exclusive. It is much more tricky to devise mutually exclusive categories in attitudinal questions. Table 2.2 shows data from a survey of working mothers with children aged under 11, who were asked to give the main reason why they had chosen to work. Looking closely at the categories in the table leads one to wonder whether categories 2 and 6, and 3 and 5, are mutually exclusive. If these pairs of categories are not exclusive, the distribution of answers between them will depend not only on the respondents' attitudes, but also on the order in which the attitude statements occur on the questionnaire, and on other irrelevant factors, making the data worthless.

Finally, the set of categories must be exhaustive. Every item must be classifiable into one of the categories. In Table 2.2 the 'other' category was included solely to make the classification exhaustive; all but one of the respondents has chosen one of the reasons provided by the researchers. Similarly, one might include in a classification of family size a last category defined as 'ten or more children'. Because of their 'catch-all' nature, very little is learnt about respondents who get classified into this kind of category, so

Table 2.2   *Main Reason for Mother with Children Choosing to Go Out to Work*

(1)	For the money	34
(2)	To get me out of the house	33
(3)	For the company	20
(4)	To use my training	11
(5)	Because I enjoy working	27
(6)	Because I hate housework	3
(7)	Other	1
	Total	129

Source: survey for a student research project.

one tries to design the classification so as to reduce the 'other' responses to a minimum. Once the categories have been chosen, and the classification scheme has been established, further decisions have to be made about the relationship between categories. As we shall see, these decisions have no less important implications for the subsequent analysis than the decisions made about the categories themselves.

Non-Metric and Metric Scales

The simplest type of classification is one in which the categories are just labelled, without any suggestion of a relationship between them. For instance, a classification by sex, in which people are categorised into 'males' and 'females', is of this type, as is the ethnic groups classification in Table 2.1. Alternatively, the categories may be ordered, or they may be based on an underlying quantitative scale, as with the measurement of age or income. The relationship existing between categories is used to define the *level of measurement* of the scale.

The most basic level of measurement is known as the *categorical* (sometimes called the *nominal*) level. Measurement at the categorical level only involves applying names to the items being measured and, thus, classifying them. For instance, measurements might be made about people's political views. Respondents to a survey would be classified according to the appropriate party, as 'Labour', 'Liberal', 'Conservative', or 'other'. The classification carries with it no implication of any ordering amongst the categories. Labour voters are not assumed to be better, bigger, or longer than Conservatives, just different.

Measurement at the *ordinal* level means that the categories are ordered or ranked. As an example, respondents to surveys are frequently asked to indicate their opinion about an attitude statement by marking whether they strongly agree, agree, are indifferent, disagree, or strongly disagree. This is measuring their attitude at the ordinal level, for the classification is into categories which are assumed to be clearly ordered. An example taken from the General Household Survey, 1973 (OPCS, 1976) of a question that yields an ordinal scale is shown in Table 2.3. It can be seen that the response categories are arranged in order from most to least satisfied. But not all ordinal scales come from attitude questions, although this is perhaps the most common source. Social class is often measured at

Table 2.3   *Question on Job Satisfaction*

Hand informant Card A
16   Which of the statements on this card comes nearest, in
your opinion, to what you think about your present
(main) job?

Very satisfied
Fairly satisfied
Neither satisfied, nor dissatisfied
Rather dissatisfied
Very dissatisfied

Source: adapted from *General Household Survey, 1973*, OPCS, 1976.

the ordinal level, as in the Registrar-General's classification of occupations mentioned above.

A feature of ordinal measurement which distinguishes it from the next higher level of measurement is that, although the categories are recognised to be ordered, no assumptions are made about the *amount* of difference between one category and the next. Indeed, it is usually meaningless to ask about the amount of difference between categories on an ordinal scale. For instance, we do not assume that someone who responds 'very satisfied' to the question about his job is twice or any other quantifiable amount more satisfied than someone who replies that he is 'fairly satisfied'. Likewise, it does not make much sense to say that occupational class II has twice as much 'classness' as class I.

Although we have been dealing with *measurement*, so far we have not used any numbers. What we have been doing is labelling categories with words such as 'very satisfied' or 'Hindu' to construct a scale, then assigning items to the categories according to measurements of some property of the items. This is sometimes described as *mapping* the property on to a scale. If there is a relationship amongst the categories (as on an ordinal scale), this should reflect the relationship amongst the items being measured. If an ordinal scale is applied to items which cannot be compared, the mapping from items to scale becomes inaccurate – the scale indicates relationships which are not actually there.

It is equally desirable to choose a scale in which the relationships between the categories reflect the full relationships between the items. For example, if one can compare and rank items on some property, a categorical scale to measure with should not be used, for one thus loses the information available from the comparisons. The mapping in this case is not inaccurate, but it is incomplete.

There are many properties of items which not only can be compared, but also added or subtracted. Common physical properties like volume and mass are of this kind. Two volumes of beer can be joined together ('added') to make a third, larger volume, for instance. To measure such properties, a scale is needed in which the category labels can be both compared and added. The most convenient kind of scale with which to do comparison *and* addition is the one made up of numbers. In such a scale, known as a *metric* scale, the category labels are ordinary numbers.

The numbers represent the *amount* of the property possessed by the items being measured. For instance, we might measure the income of individuals on a metric scale, the numbers in this case representing the number of pounds sterling which make up a salary. Or we might wish to measure the distance between respondents' homes and the nearest urban centre. Here one would be likely to use a metric scale, having units of 'miles', in which the number assigned to a respondent would represent the number of miles out of town that he or she lives.

Metric scales are mappings of properties of items on to the number system. The mapping is only appropriate if the conventional relationships between numbers in the ordinary number system have their counterparts in the relationships between items. Two of the most fundamental operations which can be carried out between numbers are comparison and addition. Hence, one ought only to map a property on to a metric scale if it is meaningful to compare and to 'add' (more formally, 'concatenate') the items being measured. To apply a metric scale to a property, therefore, we need to be sure that items can meaningfully both be compared and concatenated. For instance, incomes can be compared and also concatenated, so we can use a metric scale to measure them.

The fact that, with a metric scale, a property has been mapped on to the number system conveys the great advantage that arithmetical procedures can be performed on the category labels. For instance, addition, subtraction and multiplication (though not always division) are meaningful operations on the labels, that is, the numbers of a metric scale. Since many powerful statistical techniques depend on such arithmetical procedures, it is best to measure on a metric scale whenever possible. However, concatenation is not meaningful for many sociologically interesting properties, and for these one is confined to the use of non-metric scales.

Just as non-metric scales are divided into two types, categorical and ordinal, metric scales are also broken down into types, of which the most important is the *interval* level of measurement (the base unit often being known as the 'interval'). An interval scale has all the features of a metric scale that we have discussed. Its categories are defined in terms of a base unit of measurement. Items are then classified into the categories according to the number of base units they possess. Pounds sterling, miles, examination marks, years of age, are all examples of base units.

A second type of metric scale is the *ratio* scale. This has the properties of an interval scale with, in addition, the feature that items exist which possess nothing of the property being measured. These items are classified into a 'zero' category. For instance, households may be classified according to the number of children living in them. This is a ratio level measure, having a base unit or interval of one child, and possessing a zero category into which households with no children are placed. In contrast, social status is a concept which can in some circumstances be measured at the interval level, but which cannot be measured at the ratio level (no one has 'zero status'). Often, however, little depends on the difference between interval and ratio, and we shall usually focus only on the distinction between metric (including interval and ratio) and non-metric (including ordinal and categorical) measurements.

A couple of important points of caution need to be made about these levels of measurement. Any category may be labelled with either a name, or a number. Although applying numeric labels is often convenient, it must always be remembered that the numbers are simply a special kind of label for the categories. Only with metric measurements may one use arithmetical procedures on the numbers. Thus one could label the categories of 'religious affiliation', 1 for Protestant, 2 for Catholic and 3 for 'other'. Nevertheless it would clearly not be sensible to calculate the 'average' or 'mean' religious affiliation of a number of people. The result might be 2·75, indicating somewhere 'between' Catholic and 'other', a clearly nonsensical result. To calculate a mean, one has to perform arithmetic (multiplication) on the category numeric labels, an operation violating the logic of non-metric measurement. In contrast, it is legitimate to find the mean income of an occupational group, because in this case we are dealing with metric measurements for which the category labels relate directly to the number of intervals (pounds sterling) corresponding to those categories.

Another way of looking at this is that the numerical labels we apply to the categories of religious affiliation are arbitrary. We could alternatively have labelled them 101, 212 and 97, and these labels, though eccentric, would not be wrong. We do not have the same freedom with the income categories which must be labelled with the correct quantities of pounds, because we are using a metric scale. The categories of an ordinal scale may also be labelled with numbers, though one normally does so in a way that preserves the rank order of the categories; but again ordinary arithmetical operations may not be used on these numbers. Only comparisons are valid.

One obtains meaningless results when calculating a mean of measurements made at the categorical or ordinal level, because one is trying to use information not present in the data. Each level contains a differing amount of information, the least being in categorical level measurements and the greatest in those at the ratio level. For instance, data on the number of people classified in the categories, 'young', 'middle-aged' and 'old' has to be treated as measured at the ordinal level. To treat it as interval, would require knowledge of the number of years separating the categories, information not available from the data. No amount of statistical computation will allow us to recover this information and so raise the level of measurement from non-metric to metric.

In general, there are considerable advantages in measuring at as high a level as possible, since then as much information as possible is incorporated. However, one is sometimes forced to measure at an ordinal level, because methods of measurement able to yield interval scales have not yet been developed. Sometimes there are theoretically based reasons for regarding a measure as ordinal or categorical even though, at first sight, it appears to have been measured at the interval level. This is the case when a measurement is used as an indicator of a more fundamental, but difficult to measure concept. For instance, education is difficult to measure directly, if by 'education' one means the quantity and quality of knowledge and skill people have acquired. We may be prepared to use the number of years that respondents have attended school and other educational establishments as an indicator of education, and 'years of schooling' is obviously easy to measure at the interval level. But even so, the underlying concept, education, should be regarded as having been measured only at the ordinal level. Although the longer one stays at school, the more one may be assumed to have learnt, the relationship between years of schooling and education cannot be made more precise than this. At present few of the most important and fundamental concepts in sociology can be measured at the interval level – even though some common indicators of those concepts can be.

Another example of measurement at the ordinal level, when the data would at first glance appear to be interval, occurs in the use of 'semantic differentials'. A respondent is presented with a number of scales in the form of lines marked at each end with adjectives or *constructs* such as 'friendly' and 'unfriendly'. He is asked to indicate the degree of friendliness of some person known to him by positioning a cross on the line. This is repeated for each construct and for a number of persons. We can easily measure the positions of the crosses on the lines to yield metric measurements. But it would be unwise to analyse such data as metric, for to do so would imply that the respondent is able to construct a uniform scale between his ideas of 'friendly' and 'unfriendly' and to place his response in terms of unit intervals along the line. A more reasonable procedure would involve dividing each scale line into coarse divisions and coding the positions of the crosses according to the divisions into which they fall. The information about the precise position of the crosses on the lines would then be discarded as unreliable; only the relative ordering of the crosses would be used in the analysis. In other words, the data would be treated as ordinal-level data.

At the conclusion of the measurement process, we shall have data on the number of 'items', that is, people, events, actions, or whatever, which fall into each of the categories. We shall, then, have obtained a *frequency* for each category. These frequencies are simply counts measured at a ratio level. Therefore, there is an important distinction between the level of measurement entailed in the classification of items into categories (which may be categorical, ordinal, interval, or ratio) and the level of measurement of the counting once the classification has been performed (which is always at the ratio level).

We have discussed levels of measurement in some detail, because it is very important not to use techniques of analysis which assume one's data contains more information than it actually does. An example was given above of the worthless results obtained if a mean of the categorical variable, religious affiliation, were calculated. This was because to compute a mean, one requires information which is only available in metric data. Other procedures have been developed to measure the central tendency of measurements made on non-metric scales. The *mode* is used for categorical scales. The category containing the most items (the one in which the items occur with the greatest frequency) is the *modal category*. Table 2.4 shows data measured on a categorical scale for which the mode is the most appropriate way of measuring central tendency. Clearly the modal category is that for 'employees'.

Table 2.4   *Economic Activity of Males, 1971*

		Thousands
Economically active		
	Self-employed	1,472
	Employees	13,560
	Sick	190
	Other	662
Economically inactive		
	Students	933
	Retired	2,304
	Housewives and others	376

Source: Central Statistical Office, *Social Trends*, 1976, table 4.3, from the 1971 Census.

The *median*, the measure of central tendency for ordinal scales, is defined as that category which has half the items falling in categories within and below the median category, and half in those within and above. Table 2.5 shows data for which the median is the appropriate measure, if we assume that the categories of socioeconomic status are ordered. The median category is 'skilled manual'. Notice that the definition of the median requires that the categories can be compared and ordered (so that we can know which are 'above' and 'below' the median), but the definition of the mode does not require us to make comparisons or to know anything about the inter-relationships between categories. Hence, a median can only be obtained for scales in which comparison is meaningful (ordinal or metric), whilst the mode is available for any scale.

In a similar way one can classify all statistical measures and procedures according to the demands they make on data. Some of the more common one- and two-variable procedures are listed in Table 2.6, grouped by the type of data they require. Those in the 'metric' boxes are the best known and most widely used. This is not

Table 2.5   *Socioeconomic Profile of Local Authority Tenants, 1974*

	%
Professional and managerial	6
Intermediate and junior non-manual	14
Skilled manual, etc.	39
Semi-skilled manual, etc.	29
Unskilled	12

Source: General Household Survey, 1974, OPCS, 1977.

because most sociological data is metric. On the contrary, it is quite hard to find sociological concepts which satisfy the requirements of metric measurement. Nevertheless, researchers often have been forced into using metric procedures for lack of more appropriate ones and have had to hope that they were not thereby generating entirely spurious results.

Table 2.6   *Statistical Techniques Classified by the Levels of Measurement They Require*

	Relationship between categories	*Applicable measures of central tendency*	Two-variable procedures *Level of second variable:*	
			Categorical Ordinal	*Interval*
Level of measurement				
Categorical (nominal)	None	Mode	Loglinear analysis	
Ordinal	Ordered	Median	Loglinear analysis	Non-metric multidimensional scaling
Non-Metric				
Metric				
Interval and ratio	Ranked and mapped on to the real number system	Mean	Analysis of variance Discriminant analysis	Factor analysis Regression Canonical correlation

Regression and factor analysis, together with their cousins, path analysis and analysis of variance, were first developed not in sociology, but in disciplines such as biology, agriculture and psychology, where metric data is more easily obtainable. They were imported into sociology because of their apparent utility. Although it cannot be denied that these techniques may be applied to some sociological research problems with valuable results, their usefulness is much more restricted than is commonly supposed because of their reliance on the extra information available in metric data.

The purpose of this book is to introduce a technique which is particularly suitable for the analysis of sociological data, because it does not demand that measurements have been made using a metric scale. Loglinear analysis is most appropriately used with data measured at the categorical level, although it can also be used with ordinal data. But before we become involved in the details of this technique, we must review some basic features of cross-tabulations, the starting-point for loglinear analyses.

Summary

Measurement involves classifying items into categories, and counting the number of items falling into each category. The categories should be chosen so that they relate to a common property and are mutually exclusive and exhaustive, and so that each category includes items which can be considered to be similar for analytic purposes. The relationship between categories is described in terms of levels of measurement: either categorical (no relationship); ordinal (categories are ordered); interval (categories are based on a number scale); or ratio (the categories are based on a number scale with a true zero). The first two levels of measurement are non-metric, the latter are metric. The level of measurement of a classification indicates the amount of information it incorporates, and this determines the arithmetical and statistical procedures which may be carried out on it. The most familiar statistical techniques require metric measurement, although most sociological data is non-metric.

Further Reading

A brief, clear discussion of levels of measurement is to be found in Blalock (1979, chapter 2). Abell (1971) in chapter 4 develops the idea of measurement systems in more depths. Oppenheim (1968) is good on question design and attitude scaling.

3

Cross-Tabulations

Cross-tabulations, also called *contingency tables*, lie at the heart of most quantitative social research. The aim of the researcher, given a cross-tabulation such as Table 3.1, is to discover whether there is a relationship between the variables in it and, if there is, to find the form of that relationship. Once a relationship has been identified, the researcher can begin interpreting it to show that the data he has collected confirms or contradicts his theory. Later, we shall be principally concerned with ways of modelling relationships between variables in cross-tabulations and making inferences from the relationships found. First, however, some notation and terminology must be introduced.

Table 3.1 *Sex Preferences for Next Baby and Sex Composition of Present Family amongst Mothers Wanting Another Baby*

Mother would prefer baby to be:	Present family		
	Boy(s) only	*Girl(s) only*	*Boy(s) and girl(s)*
Boy	24	210	30
Girl	209	24	21
Don't mind	105	100	47

Source: derived from part of table 16, Cartwright, 1976.

Table 3.1 shows a simple cross-tabulation of two variables: mothers' preferences for the sex of their next child, and the sex composition of the mothers' present families. We would say there was a relationship between the two variables, if the mothers' preferences varied according to the kind of family they have at present. It is clear from a brief inspection that their preferences do, indeed, vary depending on their present family composition. On the whole, mothers with children of one sex tend to want their next child to be of the other sex, but those with both sons and daughters are more likely to have no strong preference for a boy or girl. As Cartwright (1976) notes, the relationship she found between family composition and preference for a son or daughter may have important demographic implications, if it ever became possible for people to choose the sex of their children.

Table 3.1 is an example of a cross-tabulation of just two categorical variables. Let us now look at an example of a more complex table, involving four cross-classified variables. The UK Marriage Research Centre has conducted a survey of divorcees (Thornes and Collard, 1979), and we shall use some unpublished data from this study as a continuing example of a multivariate cross-tabulation here and in Chapter 4. The kind of questions one can begin to answer, using the data of Table 3.2, are: 'Are those who say that they have had affairs whilst married also likely to admit to sex before marriage?'; 'Are divorced men and women more likely to admit to having been involved in premarital sex or adultery than those still married?'; 'Is there a difference in the willingness of the two sexes to report that they have been involved in sexual adventures?'

Table 3.2   Sex, by Reports of Experience of Premarital Sex (PMS) and Extramarital Sex (EMS), by Marital Status

		Marital status			
		Divorced		Still married	
	Reported EMS:	Yes	No	Yes	No
Sex	Reported PMS				
Women	Yes	17	54	4	25
	No	36	214	4	322
Men	Yes	28	60	11	42
	No	17	68	4	130

Source: UK Marriage Research Centre.

The data in Table 3.2 were obtained by asking around 500 randomly selected men and women who had petitioned for divorce and a similar number of married people two questions: (a) 'Before you married your (former) husband/wife, had you ever made love with anyone else?', (b) 'And during your (former) marriage, (did you have) have you had any affairs or brief sexual encounters with another man/woman?' Note that although the researchers took some precautions to put their respondents at ease and to assure them that their replies were in confidence, one should be careful not to place too much reliance on the accuracy of the answers as reports of fact. Divorcees might well have admitted to their sexual adventures more freely than those still married.

Since the analysis of cross-tabulations like Table 3.2 will be the focus of this chapter, it would be useful to begin by defining some terms to describe them. The table cross-classifies four *variables*, each of which is divided into *categories* or *levels* ('yes' and 'no', 'men' and 'women'). In this table all the variables have two categories (although in many cases, we shall have to deal with variables divided into more than two categories). Each category is identified by a *label*. Each combination of categories is represented by one square or *cell*. A cell contains a count of the number of respondents whose replies and whose sex and marital status correspond to that cell's combination of categories. Because the cells hold counts or frequencies, the table is said to be a *frequency table*. The number of variables in a table is often referred to as the table's *dimensionality*. Table 3.2 has been arranged in the square format most commonly found in the literature, although other arrangements can sometimes be clearer. Table 3.3, for example, is equivalent to Table 3.2 but has the variables rearranged so that marital status is laid out along one side with the other variables across the top.

Table 3.3   *Marital Status by Sex by Report of Pre- and Extramarital Sex (PMS and EMS)*

				Sex				
		Women				Men		
		Reported PMS				Reported PMS		
	Yes		No		Yes		No	
Marital	Reported EMS		Reported EMS		Reported EMS		Reported EMS	
Status	Yes	No	Yes	No	Yes	No	Yes	No
Divorced	17	54	36	214	28	60	17	68
Still married	4	25	4	322	11	42	4	130

Marginal Tables

If one adds together all the frequencies along the top row of Table 3.3, the result gives the total number of divorcees in the sample as a whole. Similarly, the sum of the frequencies in the bottom row is equal to the number of married people in the sample. The totals are known as *marginals*, because they are conventionally added to the table along its margin. The total numbers of women and men can be found by summing the cell frequencies in the left- and right-hand halves of the table, respectively, and by selecting the appropriate sets of cells, one can also find the totals of those responding one way or the other to the questions about pre- and extramarital sex. These totals are also known as marginals, although there is no convenient margin in Table 3.3 on which to record them.

Table 3.4   *Marginal Table of Marital Status by Sex*

	Sex	
Marital status	*Women*	*Men*
Divorced	321	173
Married	355	187

The marginals indicate the frequencies obtained by disregarding all the other variables. For instance, the marital status marginal obtained by adding along the rows represents the frequencies of married and divorced people in the sample, ignoring for the moment all the other information we possess about them. *Marginal tables* (sometimes also called just 'marginals') can be constructed by disregarding all but a few of the variables. For instance, Table 3.4 is a marginal table cross-classifying marital status and sex, in which the information on respondents' reported experience of pre- and extramarital sex has been disregarded by 'summing over' those latter two variables – that is, by adding each half-row of Table 3.3 to give the corresponding cell of the marginal table. Before reading on, you should satisfy yourself that you can obtain Table 3.4 from Table 3.3. Table 3.4 shows that there are roughly equal proportions of divorced men and women in the sample. Ten different marginal tables can be obtained by summing the data of Table 3.3 over various combinations of variables. Table 3.5 is another one of these, obtained by summing over the categories of the variable, marital status.

All the tables we have seen so far can be divided into subtables. Table 3.5, for instance, can be split into a table relating to men (the right-hand half), and a table relating to women (the left-hand half). Such subtables are known as *partial* or *conditional tables* – conditional in this instance on sex. Another way of saying much the

Table 3.5   *Marginal Table, Showing Reported Experience of Premarital Sex (PMS) by Experience of Extramarital Sex (EMS) and Sex*

	Sex			
	Women		Men	
	Reported EMS		Reported EMS	
Reported PMS	Yes	No	Yes	No
Yes	21	79	39	102
No	40	536	21	198

same thing is to describe the two tables as showing the relationship between reported experiences of pre- and extramarital sex, *controlling for* the sex of the respondent. It is evidently rather easy to become overwhelmed by the great number of marginal and partial tables one can extract from multidimensional cross-tabulations. As we shall see, loglinear analysis is a useful technique for social researchers, in part, because it provides a powerful way of describing and investigating this multitude of tables.

Since, in describing the loglinear technique, we shall need to make general statements about cross-tabulations of any dimensionality and with any number of categories per variable, we must have a convention to enable us to refer to the cells in a *generalised table*. Using this convention, we shall be able to develop a uniform method for the analysis of any cross-tabulation. The generalised table has variables A, B, C, D, and so on – an arbitrary number. We assume that variable A has a total of I categories, labelled with subscripts, thus, A_1, A_2, A_3, A_4, and so on, to the last, A_I. The categories of variable B will be B_1, B_2, B_3, and so on, to the last category B_J. The remaining variables will have categories similarly labelled $C_1 \ldots C_K$, $D_1 \ldots D_L$, and so on. The capital letters I, J, K and L represent the *number* of categories of each of the variables A, B, C and D. We shall use the corresponding lower-case letters i, j, k and l as subscripts to represent any particular category of the appropriate variable. So the value of i can range between 1, meaning the first category of variable A, to I, the last category of variable A. Similarly, j, the subscript for variable B, can take any value between 1 and J.

The frequencies in the cells of the generalised table will be represented by the symbol x, with subscripts to indicate which particular cell frequency we are considering. Table 3.6 shows a four-dimensional example of the generalised table. You will see that this example has been constructed so that it is much like Table 3.3, but with the notation replacing the data. Often we shall need to refer

Table 3.6 *Example of General Notation Applied to a Four-dimensional Table*

	D							
	D_1 C				D_2 C			
	C_1 B		C_2 B		C_1 B		C_2 B	
A	B_1	B_2	B_1	B_2	B_1	B_2	B_1	B_2
A_1	x_{1111}	x_{1211}	x_{1121}	x_{1221}	x_{1112}	x_{1212}	x_{1122}	x_{1222}
A_2	x_{2111}	x_{2211}	x_{2121}	x_{2221}	x_{2112}	x_{2212}	x_{2122}	x_{2222}

generally to any cell of a table such as Table 3.6, rather than to one particular cell. In such cases notation such as x_{ijkl} (that is, the frequency in the cell corresponding to category *i* of the variable *A*, category *j* of the variable *B*, category *k* of the variable *C* and category *l* of the variable *D*) means 'any one of the cell frequencies in a four-dimensional table'.

Recall that to construct a marginal table, all the categories of one or more variables are summed over. For instance, to obtain the marginal table of marital status by sex shown as Table 3.4, we summed over all the categories of the variables concerned with experience of pre- and extramarital sex. To arrive at the cell frequency for the top left-hand corner cell (divorced/women), we added

$$17 + 54 + 36 + 214 = 321$$

To symbolise a variable which has been summed over, we use a plus sign (+) as a subscript instead of a lower-case letter. Hence, in generalised notation the above addition would become:

$$x_{1111} + x_{1211} + x_{1121} + x_{1221} = x_{1++1}$$

The plus signs in the result represent subscripts of variables which

Table 3.7 *A Marginal Table in Generalised Notation*

	D	
A	D_1	D_2
A_1	x_{1++1}	x_{1++2}
A_2	x_{2++1}	x_{2++2}

have been summed over. Note that it is only the subscripts of the second and third variables which change from term to term as we sum over these variables' categories. Next, let us look at the frequency in the top right-hand corner cell of the marginal table. In generalised notation, the calculation is:

$$x_{1112} + x_{1212} + x_{1122} + x_{1222} = x_{1++2}$$

(make sure you follow which cells in the main table, Table 3.6, are being summed). The marginal table as a whole is shown in Table 3.7, and this is the generalised equivalent of the marital status by sex table, Table 3.5. To help make this notation for marginals completely clear, Table 3.8 reproduces Table 3.7 with the addition of all *its* marginals. See how plus signs replace the subscripts being summed over. The table total is found by summing over *all* the variables (that is, adding together all the cell frequencies), and so its notation is x_{++++}.

Table 3.8 *A Marginal Table with its Marginals*

		D	Total
A	D_1	D_2	
A_1	x_{1++1}	x_{1++2}	x_{1+++}
A_2	x_{2++1}	x_{2++2}	x_{2+++}
Total	x_{+++1}	x_{+++2}	x_{++++}

All these definitions are not very exciting and perhaps a little confusing at first sight. However, they are essential, if we are to develop methods of analysis of multivariate cross-tabulations that can be used on all tables, no matter how complex they may be. Using the notation, we shall be able to apply powerful methods which, once learnt, can be applied quite generally and in the same way to any cross-tabulation. Nevertheless, in Chapter 4, we begin in a more modest way by considering just the relationships between a pair of variables, and use that as a basis for more complicated analyses.

Further Reading

Zeisel (1958) is a good introductory guide to the construction and reading of cross-tabulations. Appendix A of Rosenberg (1968) provides a shorter treatment.

4

Association and Interaction

We have already seen that a primary concern in analysing a cross-tabulation is modelling the relationships between its variables. The relationship which might exist between two variables such as those shown in Table 4.1, is known as an *association*. In the first part of this chapter, we shall explore various ways of seeing whether there is association in a simple two-variable table. Then we consider the relationship known as *interaction*, which may be found amongst three variables.

Table 4.1   *Income by Occupation, for Respondents who Reported the Income They Earned during 1976*

	Occupation		
Income	*Manual*	*Non-manual*	*Total*
Less than $10,000	302	239	541
$10,000 or more	194	240	434
Total	496	479	975

Source: ICPSR, 1977.

Table 4.1 is a cross-tabulation of 'type of occupation' (manual or non-manual) and 'income' (divided into two categories for the sake of simplicity) from a random sample of US citizens. Is there a relationship between the two variables? To answer this question, we need first to be clear about what is meant by 'relationship'. There are several equivalent ways of thinking about the relationship between two variables. One is to see whether respondents are distributed across the categories of one variable in the same proportions regardless of the category they fall into on the other variable. Table 4.1 shows that the distribution of respondents in the two income categories differs between the two occupation categories. There are proportionately more manual than non-manual workers in the lower-income category. We can be more precise about this by drawing up a percentaged table like Table 4.2. This shows that 61 per cent of manual workers earned less than $10,000, as compared with only 50 per cent of non-manual workers. Because the distribution of respondents between income categories differs between the occupation categories, we say that there is a relationship, specifically an association, between the variables occupation and income in the sample.

Table 4.2   *Percentaged Distribution of Income, by Occupation*

Income	Manual	Occupation Non-manual	Total
Less than $10,000	61	50	56
$10,000 or more	39	50	54
	100	100	100
	(496)	(479)	(975)

Another but equivalent way of thinking about association is in terms of probabilities. There is a 61 per cent probability of a manual worker from the sample having an income below $10,000, but only a 50 per cent probability for a non-manual worker. Thus, amongst the sample, a respondent's occupation does make a difference to the probability that he or she has an income below $10,000, and this shows there is association. These two ways of viewing association are statistically equivalent, although you may find one easier to grasp than the other. Both show the existence of association between income and occupation in this data.

There is another, quicker way of telling whether there is association in tables of two variables when each variable has only two categories (namely, '2 by 2' tables). Multiply the top left-hand frequency and the bottom right-hand frequency, and divide the result by the product of the top right-hand and bottom left-hand frequencies. This gives a number known as the *cross-product ratio*, which is equal to one if there is no association. The cross-product ratio for Table 4.1 is:

$$\frac{302 \times 240}{239 \times 194} = 1 \cdot 56$$

so the variables are associated. Sometimes in loglinear analysis the cross-product ratio is called the *odds ratio*.

Although there is association in this table, its strength (the amount of association) is quite modest. The probability of earning less than $10,000 changes by only 11 per cent as one moves from the manual to non-manual category. A reason for the low degree of association can be seen from Tables 4.3 and 4.4, in which the data have been divided into two separate tables, one for men and the other for women. Tables 4.3 and 4.4 are two partial tables derived from Table 4.1, controlling for the sex of the respondent. Since all the respondents have been placed in one or other of the two partial tables, the cell by cell sums of the entries in the two partial tables equal the entries in the corresponding cells of the full table, Table 4.1.

Table 4.3   *Income by Occupation, for Male Respondents Only*

| | | Occupation | |
Income	Manual	Non-manual	Total
Less than $10,000	148	51	199
	(46%)	(25%)	
$10,000 or more	175	157	332
	(54%)	(75%)	
Total	323	208	531
	(100%)	(100%)	

Table 4.4   *Income by Occupation, for Female Respondents Only*

| | | Occupation | |
Income	Manual	Non-manual	Total
Less than $10,000	154	188	342
	(89%)	(69%)	
$10,000 or more	19	83	102
	(11%)	(31%)	
Total	173	271	444
	(100%)	(100%)	

The first thing to notice about these partial tables is that each shows a much greater degree of association between income and occupation than the full table. In other words, the differences between the distributions of income for manual and non-manual workers, keeping the men and women separate, is greater than the difference for all workers combined. Again, this is easiest to see by looking at the percentage figures. Secondly, whilst non-manual males tend to be paid over $10,000, non-manual females are relatively much worse paid. Conversely, a higher proportion of males than females in manual jobs earns $10,000 or more. This means that the associations in the two partial tables are quite different, and are almost mirror-images of each other. Summing the two partial tables to form the full table, tends to 'wash out' the opposing strong associations visible in the single-sex partial tables, and this is why quite a low level of association was found in the full table (Table 4.1).

To summarise, we have found some association in all three tables, but we have also discovered that the association between occupation and income is affected by the sex of the respondent. We conclude, therefore, that sex is an important factor in determining the association between occupation and income in the sample. Women tend to be paid less than men for doing jobs of the same kind. To distinguish the associations in these tables, the association in the partial tables is called the *partial association*, and the association in the full table is the *marginal association* ('marginal' because this table is a marginal table of the three-dimensional income by occupation by sex table).

We noted above that when two variables such as occupation and income are related, so that the level of one variable makes a difference to the distribution of respondents on the other, the relationship is termed 'association'. When three variables are related, in a way such that the association between two of them changes according to the level of the third, the relationship between the three is called *interaction*. (This statistical meaning of 'interaction' has nothing to do with the other common use of the word, in sociology and social psychology, to refer to exchanges between two or more people.) Since, as remarked above, the association between income and occupation is quite different for men and for women, there must be some interaction between income, occupation and sex. Sometimes interaction is called 'specification' (Rosenberg, 1968) because, for example, sex helps to specify the degree of association between income and occupation.

The interaction we have found can be interpreted as follows. Women tend to obtain low-paid non-manual jobs, becoming clerks, typists, nurses and shop assistants, rather than taking up the managerial and professional posts filled by men. One would always expect (within a capitalist system) that income and occupation would be associated, but the difference in the partial associations according to sex is a clear indication of women's present lack of equality of income. If in future the amount of interaction were to get smaller, this would be a sign of increasing sexual equality.

The procedure we have used in this example, first examining a cross-tabulation of two variables, then spotting changes in the degree of association between the two when one controls for a third, is called *elaboration*. Elaboration is a simple technique for analysing the mutual influence of three variables when one (for instance, sex) is clearly causally prior (that is, has a causal effect on) the other two, and it has been much used by social researchers (Rosenberg, 1968). However, it is limited to the analysis of three cross-classified variables. Since one obtains a partial table for each category of the control variable, if the control variable has more than two or three levels the comparison of partial tables quickly gets unmanageable. Moreover, in many cases it is not as clear as in our example which of the three variables is best chosen as the control variable. It is only because we know that sex may affect income and occupation, but income and occupation cannot affect sex, that it was easy to see that sex must be the variable to control.

Cross-tabulations of more than three variables, such as that concerning experience of pre- and extramarital sex in Chapter 3, cannot conveniently be analysed using elaboration, for there are just too many partial tables needing to be compared. But perhaps the most significant failing of the elaboration technique is that the researcher can proceed with the analysis without developing a clear model of the inter-relationships between his variables. To put it bluntly, elaboration allows the researcher to muddle through, picking on one or other relationship to examine, and does not force him to think clearly about what he expects to find in his data. In contrast, loglinear techniques require the formulation of models from prior theoretical expectations. These models can be developed in a systematic way to explore all the relationships in one's data.

Analysing a Two-Dimensional Table

To show how we might develop and use a model to analyse data, we return to the simplest relationship, an association between two variables, and employ some of the data on sexual experiences introduced in Chapter 3 for a further example. We shall take this example slowly, concentrating on the principles of the analysis in order to lay a foundation for the more complex examples to be discussed later. Table 4.5 is one marginal from the full table, Table 3.2, cross-tabulating reports of experiences of premarital sex with current marital status. We use a model to answer two questions: are the two variables related, and if so, how strongly.

Table 4.5   Frequency of Reporting Experience of Premarital Sex (PMS), by Marital Status

	Marital status		
Reporting PMS	Married	Divorced	Total
No	460	335	795
Yes	82	159	241
Total	542	494	1,036

The first step of the analysis is to choose a model that expresses the presumed relationship (or lack of it) between the two variables. We wish to find the simplest model which will satisfactorily represent the relationship, so we begin by seeing whether a model which involves no association between marital status and reports of premarital sex is an adequate one. This means that we should try to fit a 'model of no association'. If the model generates data similar to the data which has been collected, then we may conclude that there is indeed no relationship between the two variables. On the other hand, if the modelled data does not resemble the real data, then we must suppose that there is association between the variables, and that the likelihood of reporting experiences of premarital sex depends on one's marital status.

In terms of the ideas introduced in Chapter 1, we must compare the 'real' world represented by the data of Table 4.5 with an 'imaginary' world, represented by a table obtained using a model of no association. If the tables are identical, there is no association between the variables; if they differ, the model does not fit and the variables are associated.

Thus the second step of the analysis is to construct a table, the model table, showing what the distribution of respondents would be if there were no association between marital status and reporting premarital sex. The table must be identical to the data in all possible respects, *other* than in having no association. This is necessary in order to ensure that the 'real' and 'imaginary' worlds are the same excepting only those relationships specified in the model. In particular, the model table must include the same total number of respondents, and the same proportions of respondents must be married, and must report premarital sex. In short, the marginals of the model table must equal the marginals of the data table. The body of the model table must be filled with those frequencies which would be obtained if there were no association between the variables, since this is how we wish the 'imaginary world' to be.

The required frequencies can be calculated very simply by multiplying together the marginal entries to the right and below each cell, and dividing by the table total. For instance, the frequency for the top left cell of the model table (married; no premarital sex) must be 795 multiplied by 542 divided by 1,036. Table 4.6 shows in section (a) the results of these calculations. (Make sure that you follow how it was constructed.) This model table includes the frequencies which one would expect to obtain in an 'imaginary world', where there was no association between marital status and reporting experience of premarital sex. As a check that it does indeed show no association between the variables, one can compute the percentages across the table (shown in (b) in Table 4.6) to demonstrate that the distribution of cases is the same for the two levels of premarital sex.

Thus we now have the frequencies to be expected in an 'imaginary world', to compare with the frequencies which were actually collected in the 'real world'. If the data table (Table 4.5) and the model table were identical, the conclusion we would draw is that the two variables are not related. However, the two tables are clearly different, and this means that there is some association. Our initial model of no association is revealed to be incorrect, and we can infer

Table 4.6   Table for Model of No Association

(a) *Frequencies*

| Reporting PMS | Marital status | | |
	Married	Divorced	Total
No	416	379	795
Yes	126	115	241
	542	494	1,036

(b) *Percentaged across marital status, to show no association*

| Reporting PMS | Marital status | | |
	Married	Divorced	Total
No	52·3	47·7	100 (795)
Yes	52·3	47·7	100 (241)

that being divorced and reporting one's premarital adventures tend, in the 'real world', to go together.

The method which was used to calculate the cell entries in the model table (also called the *expected* or *fitted* table) can be expressed as

model cell entry = (product of corresponding marginals)/table total

which in the generalised notation introduced in Chapter 3 becomes

$$m_{ij} = x_{i+}x_{+j}/x_{++}$$

where m_{ij} stands for the frequency in cell i, j of the model table and x_{ij}, the frequency in the corresponding data table cell. Recall that the plus sign means sum over cells, so that, for instance, x_{i+} is the marginal obtained by summing over all values of j.

So far we have concluded only that, since the model and data tables differ, there is some association displayed in the data table. However, we may also be interested in the strength of this association. We have already met one measure of association, the cross-product ratio, but this has the disadvantage that its value can range from zero to infinity according to the amount of association in the table. A number of other measures have been designed to have the more convenient range of zero to one, zero meaning no association and one, perfect association. Several are in common use, each with its own particular merits (see Goodman and Kruskal, 1954), but we shall introduce only two.

The first, *phi*, is computed from the formula:

$$\varphi^2 = \frac{\Sigma (x_{ij} - m_{ij})^2/m_{ij}}{\Sigma m_{ij}}$$

where Σ means 'form the sum of the expression following it for all combinations of possible values of i and j', or more concisely, sum the expression calculated for each cell in the table. The formula above gives the value of phi squared, which is the form in which phi is often quoted. Phi itself is, of course, obtained by taking the square root. Phi can be seen from the formula to be based on the magnitude of the cell by cell differences between the data and model tables (that is, $x_{ij} - m_{ij}$). Phi can only be used on two-dimensional tables, in which both variables have only two levels. It is, thus, restricted to measuring association in simple '2 by 2' tables.

Let us work through an example to illustrate the meaning of the formula for phi. First, taking each cell in turn, we subtract the model table cell entry (m_{ij}) from the data table cell entry (x_{ij}), square the result and divide by the model table cell entry. For the data shown in Table 4.5, the top left-hand cell entry (x_{11}) is 460. The corresponding model table cell entry (m_{11}), from Table 4.6, is 416. Subtracting 416 from 460 gives 44; squaring and dividing by 416 gives 4·65. Similar calculations carried out for the other three cells yield for the top right cell, 5·11; for the bottom left cell, 15·4; and for the bottom right cell, 16·8. Next, the summation sign in the numerator requires us to add these four numbers, giving 42·0. Finally, we divide by the total obtained by summing all four model table cell entries (1,036) to give phi squared, 0·0404.

Another, newer and less well known measure of association is the *uncertainty coefficient*, *U*. This particular measure lends itself to the analysis of cross-tabulations using loglinear analysis, and has advantages over phi because it may be applied to tables of any dimensionality, and to tables in which the variables have more than two levels. The uncertainty coefficient is defined by:

$$U = \frac{2 \ \Sigma \ x_{ij}(\log x_{ij} - \log m_{ij})}{\Sigma \ x_{ij}(\log x_{ij} - \log m_{ij}) + \Sigma \ x_{ij}(\log x_{++} - \log m_{ij})}$$

Although it may not be so evident, the uncertainty coefficient is also based on the difference between model and data tables. However, it measures the difference on a log scale $(\log x_{ij} - \log m_{ij})$.

For Table 4.5, phi squared is equal to 0·040 and the uncertainty coefficient to 0·033. Both measures confirm that there is a small association between marital status and reporting premarital sex. Nowadays measures of association are usually calculated by computer, so it is less important to worry about the apparent complexity of their formulae than to understand the basic principles and assumptions underlying them.

Although we have found a small association between reporting premarital sex experiences and marital status in this data table, we cannot jump immediately to the conclusion that there is such an association in the population at large. The analysis we have performed has been applied only to the data from the sample of 1,036 people that was studied. It is possible, for instance, that the randomly chosen individuals who were asked about their experiences happened to include an unrepresentatively large number of promiscuous divorcees. The probability of the data being unrepresentative by chance in such a way that we could falsely find an association when none really existed can be assessed using a classical test of significance. As we shall see when turning to loglinear analysis, measures of significance are also valuable guides to the fit of models when one has a number of alternatives to select from. In the simple case of a two-dimensional table, however, the only interesting models to examine are those of 'no association' and its converse, the model of association. If we can reject the no association model, it follows that the alternative association model is the one to choose.

Chi square is the most common measure of significance (Caulcott, 1973). In the generalised notation, its formula is:

$$X^2 = \Sigma \ (x_{ij} - m_{ij})^2 / m_{ij}$$

The interpretation to be placed on the chi square value given by this formula depends on a characteristic of the model we are using, called its *degrees of freedom*. The degrees of freedom of a model is the inverse of the number of restrictions or constraints which have been imposed on the model table to make it conform with the data. One can think of the degrees of freedom as the number of ways in which the 'imaginary world' is permitted to vary from the 'real world'.

To begin with, there are as many degrees of freedom as there are cells in the model table. But in defining the model table, we imposed three constraints: first, that the overall total number of respondents is fixed to be equal to the number in the data (1,036); secondly, that the marginal of the premarital sex variable is distributed identically in both model and data tables; and thirdly, that the marital status marginal is distributed identically in both tables. The imposition of each of these constraints reduces the model table's degrees of freedom by one. Since Table 4.6 contains four cells, and we have imposed three constraints, it follows that the model has one degree of freedom remaining.

Returning now to the comparison of the data with the 'no

association' model, application of the formula above for the value of chi square gives:

$$X^2 = 42 \cdot 1$$

If one consults a table of the chi square distribution for one degree of freedom, it will be found that a value as high as this implies that the probability of selecting a sample showing association from a population, in which reported experience of premarital sex and marital status were not associated, is vanishingly small. We can, therefore, be confident that we are right in rejecting the no association model in favour of one which includes association.

Summary

Two variables are associated if the proportion of respondents in the categories of one variable varies according to the value of the other. Three variables interact if the degree of association between two of them varies according to the value of the third. Three-variable (three-dimensional) tables may be analysed using the technique of elaboration, which involves comparing the partial tables relating two variables controlling for the third, but the technique becomes clumsy if the variables are not dichotomous. A better method of analysing three and higher dimensional tables is loglinear analysis, which requires the specification of explicit models.

We illustrated the analysis of a table using a model with an example of a simple two-dimensional table. The logic lying behind this example is important, because the same logic is used in the much more complicated case of tables with three or more variables. What we did was to compare the observed data table with another table constructed on the assumption of a specified simple model. The model was arranged to mirror the data in all respects, except that it did not include any association between the variables. This was achieved by ensuring that the model table's marginals were kept the same as those of the data table. We decided whether the model fitted the data using an inferential test, the chi square test. The magnitude of the association was measured with phi, or the uncertainty coefficient, which expressed the extent of the deviation of the observed table from the model table. We shall follow essentially the same course of argument in Chapter 5 on turning to analyse three-dimensional tables, using loglinear analysis.

Further Reading

The concept of association between variables is treated in most texts on social statistics. Loether and McTavish (1974, part III) is especially recommended; part IV also explains elaboration and interaction clearly. Longer presentations of the method of elaboration are to be found in Rosenberg (1968) and Babbie (1973). Caulcott (1973) provides a very thorough explanation of chi square values. Blalock (1979), in appendix 1, includes a short 'refresher' on the algebra of summations and logarithms for those whose mathematics is a little rusty.

5

Loglinear Analysis

As we saw in Chapter 4, modelling a two-variable table is fairly easy. As soon as more variables are introduced, however, complications arise simply because there are more relationships to be considered. In a three-dimensional table there may be associations between each of the pairs of variables as well as interaction between all of them. In four- and five-dimensional tables the number of possible relationships multiplies alarmingly. Fortunately, once one has understood how to use loglinear models with three-dimensional tables, extension of the technique to more complex ones is straightforward.

Table 5.1 is a three-dimensional table, relating the variables occupational class, tenure and voting amongst a sample of men in Banbury in 1967. The respondents classified in this table were asked to state their occupation (used as an indicator of class measured on a version of the Registrar-General's scale), whether and how they owned or rented their home (tenure) and how they voted in the last election.

As was mentioned in Chapter 4, interaction is said to occur when the degree of association between two variables differs between the categories of a third. For instance, there is interaction in Table 5.1 if the magnitude of the association between class and tenure amongst those voting Conservative (the top half of the table) is not the same as the magnitude of the association between these two variables amongst those voting Labour (the bottom half). This is the meaning of interaction in statistical terms. But how should one interpret interaction in sociological terms? The authors of the report in which the table was published interpret it as follows:

Property ownership, including domestic property, and the work situation have, since Marx and Weber, been thought of as bases for class formation and for political action. Voting at the last

Table 5.1   *Occupational Class, Tenure and Voting amongst Economically Active Men in Banbury and District, 6 per cent Sample, 1967*

Voted Conservative

		Tenure		
Occupational class	*Own, outright*	*Own, on mortgage*	*Rented, privately*	*Rented, from council*
I and II	35	63	22	5
IIIa, IVa	18	29	18	16
IIIb	12	30	16	24
IVb	9	12	8	17
V	5	1	5	3

Voted Labour

		Tenure		
Occupational class	*Own, outright*	*Own, on mortgage*	*Rented, privately*	*Rented, from council*
I and II	5	14	3	10
IIIa, IVa	4	9	4	14
IIIb	3	44	83	42
IVb	7	18	14	45
V	0	2	5	21

Source: derived from Stacey *et al.*, 1975, table 4.1.

election may be taken as one indicator of political belief and action. [Table 5.1] suggests that there does appear to be a relationship between property ownership, higher occupational status and Conservative voting ... Those who own outright are the most Conservative category and include over 80 percent in all classes from skilled manual and above. Among those who rent privately or who own subject to mortgage it is only in the non-manual categories that there is a large Conservative majority. Those who rent from the Council are most inclined to vote Labour, and this is true even if they are in non-manual categories. It seems, therefore, that house tenure and occupational status combined account for more of the variation in voting than either taken separately. (Stacey *et al.*, 1975, p. 41)

The suggestion in the last sentence is that the data of Table 5.1 includes statistical interaction. Voting behaviour depends on type of tenure and class. But, in addition, the magnitude of the relationship between voting and tenure is affected by class. It is the variation in association between tenure and vote according to class that is meant when one says that the table displays interaction. The consequence of this interaction is that the probability of voting Conservative depends not only on the independent effects of type of home tenure and class position, but also on the effect of these two influences in *combination*.

In fact, if there is interaction, it will be found that not only does the association between tenure and vote depend on class, but also that the association between class and vote depends on tenure, and the association between class and tenure depends on vote. This is because interaction is a 'symmetrical' property: if the association between two variables depends on a third, then the association between each of the other pairs of variables will also depend on the remaining variable.

We shall introduce loglinear analysis by discovering whether it is right to suppose that Table 5.1 does reveal the presence of interaction. We shall construct a model table which shows *no*

Table 5.2   *Three Marginal Tables from the Banbury Data (Table 5.1)*

(a) *Marginal table of occupational class by vote*

	Vote	
Occupational class	Conservative	Labour
I and II	125	32
IIIa, IVa	81	31
IIIb	82	172
IVb	46	84
V	14	28

(b) *Marginal table of tenure by vote*

	Vote	
Tenure	Conservative	Labour
Own, outright	79	19
Own, on mortgage	135	87
Rented, privately	69	109
Rented, from council	65	132

(c) *Marginal table of occupational class by tenure*

		Tenure		
Occupational class	Own, outright	Own, on mortgage	Rented, privately	Rented, from council
I and II	40	77	25	15
IIIa, IVa	22	38	22	30
IIIb	15	74	99	66
IVb	16	30	22	62
V	5	3	10	24

interaction, then compare this table with the Banbury data to see if they are the same. If the model and data tables are similar, we shall have developed a simpler model to fit the data than the original study assumed was necessary. Moreover, we shall have shown that there is in fact no interaction in the data, and therefore that the study was wrong in arguing that occupational class and tenure have a joint effect on voting behaviour over and above their separate influences. The aim of this example is to illustrate the principles underlying loglinear analysis. Although here we shall work through it step by step, in practice all the calculation would be carried out using a computer.

In Chapter 4, we constructed a model of 'no association' by fixing the marginals to be the same in both data and model tables. We can do the same to calculate a model to compare with Table 5.1. However, with three-dimensional tables, we have available not only the marginals for each variable on its own, but also marginal tables showing the relationships between pairs of variables. The three marginal tables which can be derived from Table 5.1, for the pairs of variables [class, vote], [tenure, vote] and [class, tenure] are shown in Table 5.2.

We now need to compute the model table frequencies such that the model table has the same marginal tables as the data marginal tables of Table 5.2. This was an easy step for the model of 'no association' calculated in Chapter 4, since it merely involved applying the formula

$$m_{ij} = x_{i+} x_{+j} / x_{++}$$

for each model table cell in turn. Unfortunately, calculation of model table frequencies is not so straightforward when one is dealing with a model of 'no interaction', since a standard formula does not exist in this case. However, although there is no formula, there is a method or 'algorithm' which can be used, known as *iterative proportional scaling*. This can best be explained with an analogy which will be familiar to those who do household repairs.

One way to mix the kind of plaster which is used for filling cracks in walls is to obey the instructions on the packet that specify how much water is to be added to how much powder. But the way most people do it is to add a little water to some powder, mix them together and test to see whether the result has the right consistency. If it is too dry, some more water is added, or if it is too wet, some more powder. Then the mixture is stirred and tested again. This goes on until the balance of powder to water seems right. The advantage of this method is that one is more or less bound to get to the correct mixture eventually, provided only that one adds a moderate and decreasing amount of water or plaster at each stage. Moreover, one can make up the plaster, even if the instructions on the packet have been lost.

Making plaster like this is an example of an *iterative* procedure. Iterative procedures are also useful in data analysis both for finding model table frequencies, and for other kinds of numerical calculation, such as some kinds of least-squares and multidimensional scaling routines. The essential elements of an iterative procedure are:

(1)   a guess at a solution is made (for example, some plaster and a little water);
(2)   the guess is tested to see whether it is good enough (the mixture's consistency is checked), and if it is, this guess is the solution;
(3)   the guess is improved (a little more water or powder is added);
(4)   steps 2–4 are repeated until a satisfactory solution is discovered in step 2.

The great advantage of iterative methods is that they can be used when there is no formula available (cf. the lost instructions on the packet).

To calculate the frequencies for a model of 'no interaction', a guess is first made at a solution. For simplicity of calculation, this first guess is usually a table in which every cell frequency is equal to one. It does not matter that this first guess is almost certainly a very poor one; the iterative method will soon improve it. That was step 1: make a guess at a solution. Next, we must test the solution to see whether it is an adequate one (step 2). The test used is whether the marginals of the guessed table are the same as those in the data table. If they are, the desired model table has been found; if not, the guess must be improved (step 3).

Progress so far is shown in section (a) in Table 5.3. The right-hand table is the class by tenure marginal from the first guess. It is to be compared with the corresponding data marginal shown below it. Since the two marginals are clearly quite different, the solution in (a) in the table is not satisfactory and must be improved. The improvement is performed by proportionately scaling the frequencies, that is, multiplying each of them by the ratio of the data to solution marginal-table entries. For instance, the second-guess table's top right frequency is

$$[\text{first-guess table's frequency}] \times [\text{data marginal entry}]$$
$$[\text{first-guess marginal entry}]$$

$$= \frac{1 \times 40}{2}$$

$$= 20 \cdot 0$$

Carrying out the scaling for all the table frequencies yields the solution in (b), the second guess. The scaling formula ensures that the class by tenure marginal table from the second guess is exactly equal to the data marginal, as desired. However, the other two marginals may not, and probably won't, be correct. The first guess was checked and improved with the class by tenure marginal; the second guess will be improved in the same way, but using the class by vote marginal to yield the third guess (section (c) in Table 5.3). The third guess will be compared with the remaining marginal (tenure by vote); the fourth (section (d) in Table 5.3) with the class by tenure marginal like the first; and so on. The iterations continue until all three marginals from the solution match the marginals from the data, either precisely or sufficiently closely for any differences to be unimportant. The order in which the marginal tables are used in the calculation makes no difference to the result. The iterative scaling procedure almost always converges to a solution, usually within three or four cycles. It may seem laborious, but in practice it is carried out by computer, using a program such as those described in Chapter 12.

The model table one gets by continuing the process begun in Table 5.3 is shown in Table 5.4. This table has the same marginals as the data table (Table 5.1), and is the table of frequencies one would obtain if there were no interaction between class, tenure and vote. Tables 5.1 (the data) and 5.4 (the model) are different, although there is a certain similarity in the cell frequencies. This shows that the original conclusion from this data, that there is interaction, was correct (though the interaction is not very strong). Later, we shall be able to quantify the amount of interaction that is present, but for the

Table 5.3   *Iterative Scaling on the Data in Table 5.1*

The data table (Table 5.1 rearranged, with the labels omitted to save space)

35·0	63·0	22·0	5·0		5·00	14·0	3·0	10·0
18·0	29·0	18·0	16·0		4·00	9·0	4·0	14·0
12·0	30·0	16·0	24·0		3·00	44·0	83·0	42·0
9·0	12·0	8·0	17·0		7·00	18·0	14·0	45·0
5·0	1·0	5·0	3·0		0·00	2·0	5·0	21·0

(a) *First guess at a solution*

1	1	1	1	1	1	1	1
1	1	1	1	1	1	1	1
1	1	1	1	1	1	1	1
1	1	1	1	1	1	1	1
1	1	1	1	1	1	1	1

Class by tenure marginal from first guess

2	2	2	2
2	2	2	2
2	2	2	2
2	2	2	2
2	2	2	2

Class by tenure marginal from data

40·0	77·0	25·0	15·0
22·0	38·0	22·0	30·0
15·0	74·0	99·0	66·0
16·0	30·0	22·0	62·0
5·0	3·0	10·0	24·0

(b) *Second guess at a solution*

20·0	38·5	12·5	7·5		20·0	38·5	12·5	7·5
11·0	19·0	11·0	15·0		11·0	17·0	11·0	15·0
7·5	37·0	49·5	33·0		7·5	37·0	49·5	33·0
8·0	15·0	11·0	31·0		8·0	15·0	11·0	31·0
2·5	1·5	5·0	12·0		2·5	1·5	5·0	12·0

Class by vote marginal from second guess

78·5	78·5
56·0	56·0
127	127
65·0	65·0
21·0	21·0

Class by vote marginal from data

125	32·0
81·0	31·0
82·0	172
46·0	84·0
14·0	28·0

Table 5.3—Continued

(c) *Third guess at a solution*

								Tenure by vote marginal from third guess	
31·8	61·3	19·9	11·9	8·15	15·7	5·10	3·06	59·9	38·1
15·9	27·5	15·9	21·7	6·09	10·5	6·09	8·30	124	97·7
4·84	23·9	32·0	21·3	10·2	50·1	67·0	44·7	78·9	99·1
5·66	10·6	7·78	21·9	10·3	19·4	14·2	40·1	84·8	112
1·67	1·0	3·33	8·0	3·33	2·0	6·67	16·0		

Tenure by vote
marginal from data

79·0	19·0
135	87·0
69·0	109
65·0	132

(d) *Fourth guess at a solution*

42·0	66·6	17·4	9·15	4·07	14·0	5·60	3·60
21·0	29·8	13·9	16·6	3·04	9·37	6·70	9.78
6·38	25·9	28·0	16·3	5·07	44·6	73·7	52·6
7·46	11·5	6·81	16·8	5·16	17·3	15·6	47·2
2·20	1·09	2·92	6·13	1·66	1·78	7·33	18·8

Table 5.4   *Model Table for Model of 'No Interaction' Fitted to Banbury Data*

Voted Conservative

Occupational class	Own, outright	Own, on mortgage	Rented, privately	Rented, from council
		Tenure		
I and II	36·3	61·7	17·4	9.64
IIIa, IVa	19·6	29·2	14·4	17·9
IIIb	9·36	29·8	27·5	15·3
IVb	10·4	13·0	6·68	15·9
V	3·30	1·32	3·10	6·28

Voted Labour

Occupational class	Own, outright	Own, on mortgage	Rented, privately	Rented, from council
		Tenure		
I and II	3·68	15·3	7·61	5·36
IIIa, IVa	2·42	8·83	7·65	12·1
IIIb	5·64	44·2	71·5	50·7
IVb	5·55	17·0	15·3	46·1
V	1·70	1·68	6·90	17·7

moment it can be said that class and type of tenure together have some, but not much more, effect on voting behaviour than either considered separately.

Now that we have a model table, it can be used to provide a numerical illustration of the effect of interaction. For clarity, let us look at only one small portion of the model table, at those cells concerned with those who rent privately or from the council. For the 'top' classes, I and II, we can measure the association between the kind of landlord (private or council) and vote by calculating the cross-product ratio for the '2 by 2' subtable with cell entries: 17·4 and 9·64 (the Conservatives), and 7·61 and 5·36 (the Labour voters):

$$\frac{17\cdot4 \times 5.36}{9\cdot64 \times 7\cdot61} = 1\cdot27$$

Now look at the four corresponding cells for class V. These cell frequencies (3·10, 6·28, 6·90 and 17·7) can be slotted into another '2 by 2' table, showing the association between kind of landlord and vote amongst class V respondents. The cross-product ratio for this table is:

$$\frac{3\cdot10 \times 17\cdot7}{6\cdot28 \times 6\cdot90} = 1\cdot27$$

hence it is the same as for the class I and II table, because there is no interaction in the model. Repeating these calculations for the frequencies in the data table, gives a cross-product ratio of 14·7 for classes I and II, and 7 for class V, the two values differing, because the data table includes interaction.

In this example, we have been developing a model starting from the assumption that class, tenure and vote were associated, but did not interact. In the next illustration of loglinear analysis, the most obvious model to examine will be one that involves not three, but only two associations, with again no interaction. Table 5.5 is also taken from the Banbury study, this time being a cross-tabulation of occupational class, sex and voting behaviour. Occupational class has been divided in this table into only two categories: manual and non-manual, since this is how the data was presented in the Banbury study.

Table 5.5   *Voting Labour or Conservative, by Sex and Occupational Class, for Banbury and District 6 per cent Sample, 1967*

Vote*	Conservative		Labour	
Occupational	Sex†		Sex	
class	Male	Female	Male	Female
Non-manual	140	152	50	50
Manual	109	136	215	159

* Respondents voting Liberal (52, 6 per cent of total sample of 891) or not voting (220, 25 per cent of sample) excluded from table.

† Single women classified by their own occupation; those ever married by their husbands' occupation.

Source: derived from Stacey *et al.*, 1975, table XV.

The previous example showed, if indeed further evidence is needed, that the class one belongs to influences the way one votes. Sex and political persuasion are also related, women having traditionally been more likely to vote Conservative, regardless of their class position. A model to fit the data in Table 5.5 would, therefore, certainly need to allow for associations between class and vote, and sex and vote. Note that each of these associations is presumed to exist independently of the influence of the third variable. For instance, to say that class and vote are associated means that men's voting behaviour depends on their class position, and likewise that women's voting depends on their class.

It is more difficult to decide whether to include a relationship between class and sex in the model. The issue is complicated by Stacey's decision to categorise all married women, employed or not, by the occupation of their husbands. Since the majority of the female respondents (about 77 per cent) were married, most women were actually classified by their husbands' occupation. The effect of this would be to reduce considerably any possible relationship between class and sex. It is, therefore, quite likely that one would find no association between these variables in Table 5.5.

These considerations, together with our aim of using the simplest possible model which fits the data acceptably well, suggest that we should first try one in which only class and vote, and sex and vote are associated. In this model class would be independent of sex amongst the Conservatives, and the same would be true amongst the Labour voters. As before the necessary model table frequencies can be computed using iterative proportional scaling.

The model is designed so that the two associations which are to be included in it are fixed to be the same as those in the data. This is achieved by ensuring that the marginal tables for class by vote and sex by vote are the same in both data and model tables. Likewise, the total number of respondents, and the marginals for each of the three variables must be the same in both data and model tables. However, the association between class and sex in the model table must not be the same as in the data; on the contrary, the frequencies in the model table must be arranged to give zero association between these variables in each (Conservative and Labour) partial table.

Because we only require two of the marginal tables to be the same in the data and the model tables, we scale with respect to these two only. First, the guessed solution is scaled using the class by vote marginal, the resulting second guess is scaled using the sex by vote marginal, the third guess is scaled using the class by vote table again, and so the iterations continue, until the model table's class by vote and sex by vote marginals equal those of the data table. Because the class by sex marginal was not used in the scaling, the iterative procedure automatically yields frequencies which show no partial associations between this pair of variables.

Table 5.6   *Model Table for Vote, by Class and Sex, for a Model of No Interaction and No Association between Class and Sex*

Vote	Conservative		Labour	
Occupational	Sex		Sex	
class	Male	Female	Male	Female
Non-manual	135	157	56	44
Manual	114	131	209	165

The result of iterative scaling in this way is shown in Table 5.6. Neither of the partial tables of class by sex controlling for vote display any association, as required by the model specification. The marginals from the data and the model tables are compared in Table 5.7, where one can see that the first two pairs, class by vote, and sex by vote, are indeed identical, but the class by sex marginals differ slightly, not having been forced to be the same by the scaling procedure.

It is important to note here that the fact that the *partial* tables for class by sex, controlling for vote, show no association does not mean that the class by sex *marginal* table will also show no association. The amount of marginal association depends not only on the partial

Table 5.7 *Marginal Tables for Vote by Class by Sex*

	Data			Model	
Class by vote					
	Vote			Vote	
Class	*Conservative*	*Labour*	*Class*	*Conservative*	*Labour*
Non-manual	292	100		292	100
Manual	245	374		245	374
Sex by vote					
	Vote			Vote	
Sex	*Conservative*	*Labour*	*Sex*	*Conservative*	*Labour*
Male	249	265		249	265
Female	288	209		288	209
Class by sex					
	Sex			Sex	
Class	*Male*	*Female*	*Class*	*Male*	*Female*
Non-manual	190	202		191	201
Manual	324	295		323	296

associations, but also on the other associations in the table. We shall return to the distinction between partial and marginal associations in Chapter 8.

Now that we have a table (Table 5.6) based on a model of no interaction and no association between class and sex, we can compare it with the data of Table 5.5. A comparison by eye shows that the two tables do differ, but not a great deal. It is not obvious from inspection whether the model table is sufficiently similar to the data table for one to conclude that the model is an adequate one. This judgement must be made by calculating a measure of the difference between the tables like the chi square statistic used in Chapter 4. Such a measure will be introduced in Chapter 6 after a few more features of loglinear analysis have been discussed. If one were to use that measure, however, one would find that according to the conventional criterion of fit, the model we have developed does mirror the data to an adequate degree. It can be inferred, therefore, that there is no significant association between class and sex in the data, just as we had initially supposed.

One further point needs to be made before we leave this example. We assumed when we set up the model that there is an association between sex and vote. We might have been incorrect about this, but even if we were the model would still have fitted the data. The model was constructed to mirror precisely the association between these two variables, no matter how small or large that association might be. If in fact the association in the data had been zero, then that too would have been reproduced in the model. Consequently, the fact that we included an association between sex and vote in the model, and the model fits, does not prove that this association exists.

One could next try fitting another model, one in which the association between sex and vote as well as the association between class and sex were explicitly omitted. Indeed, this would be a useful next step in analysing the data. If the reduced model seemed to fit, one could try removing the class by vote relationship. In this way, we work towards the simplest model which fits the data, omitting unnecessary relationships. Later it will be seen how the process of model selection can be systematised, but first there is a more thorough discussion of how one judges whether one model fits better than another.

Summary

Loglinear analysis is used to construct a table which includes only those relationships specified in a model. The resulting table can then be compared with the data table to see whether the model is a good one. Model table frequencies can be calculated using a method known as iterative proportional scaling. This method generates a table in which some specified marginals are fixed to be identical to those in the data table, whilst others are left unconstrained. The fixed marginals are those which correspond to the relationships included in the model to be examined.

Further Reading

The most complete text on loglinear analysis is Bishop, Fienberg and Holland (1975); their chapters 2 and 3 cover the material in the present chapter, but with more mathematics. Davis (1973) includes another example of iterative proportional scaling worked step by step.

6

Choosing and Fitting Models

No less than nineteen models can be constructed to compare with a three-dimensional cross-tabulation. It is clearly desirable to have a way of deciding which is the most appropriate for describing a particular data table. One also needs a succinct notation to distinguish one model from another. In this chapter, we first look at the range of models which can be fitted to a three-dimensional table and how they may be described, then discuss ways of choosing between them.

In Chapter 5 the construction of two models was demonstrated: a 'no interaction' model and a 'no interaction and no association between one pair of variables' model. The 'no interaction' model was computed by keeping the three marginal tables corresponding to each of the three pairs of variables the same in both model and data tables. Symbolically, we can refer to this model as:

$$[A, B] [B,C] [C,A]$$

where A, B and C are the three variables. Each of the pairs of variables in brackets corresponds to one of the marginals kept the same in model and data. This notation makes it clear why the 'no interaction' model is alternatively called the 'pairwise association' model. Using this model, we are in effect comparing the 'real world' with an 'imaginary world', in which there may be association between each pair of the variables A, B, and C, but no interaction. The associations between the pairs of variables has been carried over from the 'real world' to the 'imaginary world' by ensuring that their marginal tables are the same. The marginal tables can be thought of as encapsulating the associations between their variables. Keeping the marginal tables identical in both model and data tables, builds these associations into the model. So, to construct a model with only some associations the same as in the data, one needs only to arrange for the corresponding marginal tables to be identical in both tables, leaving the remaining marginals unconstrained.

This was illustrated in the second example, in which we constructed a model which carried the associations between class and vote, and sex and vote over from the 'real world', but which had no association between class and sex. The model was built by scaling, so that only two of the three marginal tables were identical in both data and model. The remaining marginal, that for class by sex, was allowed to differ from the corresponding data marginal. This model can be referred to symbolically as:

$$[A,B] \, [B,C]$$

if the association between A and C is the one set to zero (for instance, class by sex).

We can now write down in a convenient form some of the models which can be constructed to compare with a three-dimensional table. The six most important are given in Table 6.1. The interaction model $[A,B,C]$ is the model we might develop for an 'imaginary world', in which there *was* interaction between A, B, and C. The notation implies that the 'marginal' to be kept the same in both model and data is the 'marginal' table relating all three variables. Because the table relating all three variables is the data table itself, this 'marginal' table is not really a marginal at all. Since model tables are computed by making the specified marginal table the same as in the data, this model table is easy to find: it is an exact copy of the data table. It follows that the interaction model for a three-dimensional table *always* fits the data perfectly. (This is not true, if one fits an interaction model to a data table of more than three variables.)

Table 6.1   *Models That Can Be Fitted to a Data Table Cross-tabulating Variables A, B and C*

$[A,B,C]$	interaction
$[A,B][B,C][A,C]$	no interaction, pairwise association
$[A,B][B,C]$	no interaction, no association between A and C
$[A,B][A,C]$	no interaction, no association between B and C
$[B,C][A,C]$	no interaction, no association between A and B
$[A][B][C]$	no association

There is, thus, little point in using the interaction model to examine a three-dimensional table. Similarly, there is little to be gained by comparing a two-dimensional data table against an association model (whose model table is a copy of the data table). This is why we did not bother to fit such a model when investigating the relationship between marital status and reported experience of premarital sex in Chapter 4. The result of the comparison is a foregone conclusion – it would fit exactly. Models like these which will predictably 'fit' the data are known as *saturated* models and are of little practical use in loglinear analysis.

We have already discussed the pairwise association model and the models which omit one association. The remaining model listed in Table 6.1, [A] [B] [C], is the no association model for a three-dimensional table. This is the model corresponding to an 'imaginary world', in which none of the variables are associated with any of the others. Its model table is calculated by requiring that the marginal of each individual variable remain the same in model and data tables, whilst allowing the marginal tables of A by B, B by C, and C by A to differ. By way of example, Table 6.2 shows the model table for the

Table 6.2   *Model Table for Model of 'No Association' Fitted to Banbury Data*

Voted Conservative

Occupational class	Own, outright	Own, on mortgage	Rented, privately	Rented, from council
		Tenure		
I and II	11·1	25·1	20·1	22·3
IIIa, IVa	7·91	17·9	14·4	15·9
IIIb	17·9	40·6	32·6	36·1
IVb	9·18	20·8	16·7	18·5
V	2·97	6·72	5·39	5·96

Voted Labour

Occupational class	Own, outright	Own, on mortgage	Rented, privately	Rented, from council
		Tenure		
I and II	11·1	25·0	20·1	22·2
IIIa, IVa	7·89	17·9	14·3	15·9
IIIb	17·9	40·5	32·5	35·9
IVb	9·15	20·7	16·6	18·4
V	2·96	6·70	5·37	5·94

Banbury data on class by tenure by vote, using the no association model

[Class] [Tenure] [Vote]

This table shows the frequencies which would be found in an 'imaginary world', in which none of the three variables were related to any of the others. Since we have already demonstrated the presence of interaction in this data, it comes as no surprise that this table and the data (Table 5.1) are obviously very different. A little arithmetic would prove that, as required by the model specification, the individual marginals for each of the three variables are the same in this table and the data.

We have made the point that including a two-variable marginal like [A,B] in a model means that the association between these two variables is identical in the model and data tables. Similarly, an interaction can be reproduced by specifying the marginal [A,B,C] in the model. In much the same way, a single-variable marginal, [A] for instance, carries over from the data to the model what is called the *main effect* of that variable. The main effect measures the distribution of respondents across the categories of the marginal of a variable. Accordingly, a variable with a marginal in which each cell contains the same value has no main effect.

Main effects, therefore, play a similar role for single variables as associations do for pairs of variables, and interactions for three variables. It is rare, however, for one to be directly interested in main effects. Their importance for loglinear analysis lies in the fact that one usually only builds models in which all the main effects are incorporated. To do otherwise, would be to construct models in which respondents were distributed equally across the categories of one or more variables, a quite unrealistic assumption for most social science data.

As an example, suppose we wanted to fit a model to the Banbury data in which only class and vote were to be associated, independently of type of tenure. The appropriate model would then be:

[Class, Vote] [Tenure]

the marginal of tenure being included to ensure that its main effect was retained in the model table. The model [A] [B] [C] is often called the 'main effect' model instead of the 'no association' model, because it is the model in which only main effects are present. When we calculated the 'no interaction' model, we ensured that the marginal tables

[Class, Tenure] [Class, Vote] and [Tenure, Vote]

were the same in model and data tables. In doing this, without explicitly noting the fact we also arranged for the marginals of each of the variables class, tenure and vote to be identical in both tables and, thus, for the main effects of these variables to be carried over into the model. For instance, since the class marginal is just the sum of the cell entries across the categories of vote in the class by vote marginal table, making the class by vote marginal from the model table equal to the corresponding marginal from the data automatically ensures that the marginal for class is the same in both. The same applies to the marginals of tenure and vote, which are also fixed to be the same as soon as we make the marginal tables including these variables the same.

Generalising from this example, we can see that specifying that a marginal table is to be included in a model has the consequence that the model must also include all those marginals which are themselves marginals to that marginal table. For instance, the model specified by

$$[A,B] [C]$$

not only sets the marginal table A by B and the marginal for variable C, but also the marginals of variables A and B to be the same in model and data. We could, in fact, write the model above more fully as:

$$[A,B] [A] [B] [C]$$

Likewise, the pairwise association (no interaction) model can either be written as

$$[A,B] [B,C] [A,C]$$

or as

$$[A,B] [B,C] [A,C] [A] [B] [C]$$

and these two forms are entirely equivalent.

Those marginals which can be derived from a particular marginal table are known as its *lower-order relatives*. Table 6.3 lists the lower-order relatives of each of the marginal tables which can be obtained from a three-dimensional table. Since including a marginal in a model means that all its lower-order relatives are also included, not any combination of marginals can be used to specify a model. For instance, a model cannot readily be constructed which includes the marginal table [A,B], but which does not also include the marginal [A]. This is because [A] is a lower-order relative of [A,B], and is therefore automatically added to the model when [A,B] is specified. In fact, this restriction on the form of models holds only if iterative scaling is used to calculate the model table frequencies. Models in which some lower-order relatives are omitted can be calculated using other more complex methods, but we shall confine discussion in this book to those which include lower-order relatives, the class of models known as *hierarchical* models.

Table 6.3   *Examples of Lower-Order Relatives*

Marginal	Marginal's lower-order relatives
[A,B,C]	[A,B][B,C][A,C][A][B][C]
[A,B]	[A][B]
[B,C]	[B][C]
[A,C]	[A][C]
[A]	none
[B]	none
[C]	none

This chapter began with a partial list (Table 6.1) of the models which could be compared with a three-dimensional data table. This list can now be extended to include models with main effect terms, to give the complete set of nineteen hierarchial models (Table 6.4). Note that each model is specified using the minimum number of marginals, that is, by omitting all lower-order relatives. Models specified in this way are said to be defined in terms of their *sufficient statistics*.

Choosing a Model

With nineteen models to choose from when analysing a three-dimensional table and considerably more for tables of greater dimensionality, it is clear that some way of selecting the most

Table 6.4   *Models for a Three-dimensional Table, Cross-classifying*
Variables A, B and C

(1)	$[A,B,C]$
(2)	$[A,B][B,C][A,C]$
(3)	$[A,B][B,C]$
(4)	$[A,B][C,A]$
(5)	$[B,C][C,A]$
(6)	$[A,B][C]$
(7)	$[B,C][A]$
(8)	$[C,A][B]$
(9)	$[A,B]$
(10)	$[B,C]$
(11)	$[C,A]$
(12)	$[A][B][C]$
(13)	$[A][B]$
(14)	$[A][C]$
(15)	$[B][C]$
(16)	$[A]$
(17)	$[B]$
(18)	$[C]$
(19)	grand mean

Note:

The grand mean model, in which no model marginal is constrained, is introduced in Chapter 7.

appropriate one is a necessity. So far, we have chosen models by making assumptions about the likely relationships between the variables concerned. After calculating the model table, we have compared it with the data by making a rough cell by cell examination by eye. For a more formal method of checking the fit of a model and comparing it with the fit of other models, a test of significance can be used.

In classical inferential statistics, tests of significance are used to ascertain whether a statement based on the analysis of a sample (of respondents, for instance) can be generalised to a wider population. However, the logic of these tests makes two strong assumptions: first, that the sample from which one has obtained data is a random sample from a specific population, and secondly, that just one hypothesis, formulated beforehand, is being tested. In most social science research, neither of these assumptions holds good. Even when a sample has been drawn using a random procedure, it is rare for the generalisations made from the data to be confined strictly to the population from which the sample has been selected. For instance, the Banbury study from which the data analysed in

Chapter 5 was taken used a 6 per cent random sample of Banburians. Nevertheless, the interest of the authors of the book was not confined to the social structure of Banbury. Banbury was used simply as a case study, and the authors' concerns were very much wider, as evidenced by their introductory statement that an

> important focus was the fate of the traditional society. It had undoubtedly been under challenge around 1950: had it survived, and in what form? In the 'Myth of Community Studies', Stacey outlined conditions under which a 'local social system' might develop and might be destroyed or changed. Banbury in the sixties provided an interesting test case of these ideas. (Stacey *et al.*, 1975, p. 4)

Moreover, Stacey *et al.* (1975) in the course of their discussion make frequent comparisons with the results of other community studies, mainly of small towns in the USA. It seems, therefore, that the 'population' about which these authors wished to contribute knowledge might reasonably be said to include those resident in urban communities undergoing change from more traditional social structures, worldwide, not just those in Banbury in 1967. The authors are certainly not unique in wishing to make broader generalisations from their data than the sampling procedure they used would seem to warrant. Moreover, social science would be immeasurably impoverished if researchers did feel constrained to restrict their conclusions solely to the samples they had studied.

Social science would also be much hindered if researchers were forced to test one, and only one, hypothesis on the data they had collected. Instead, one normally uses one's carefully gathered data to maximum effect, examining numerous ideas by repeatedly testing them on the same data. However, the consequence of this exploratory approach to analysis is that tests of significance lose their original meaning, and one cannot rely on the probabilities they generate as indicators of the generalisability of the hypotheses being tested.

Nevertheless, tests of significance do have an invaluable role in loglinear analysis, for they provide the most convenient means of quantifying the comparison of a model table with data. We saw in Chapter 4 that a chi square test of significance yields a probability figure which summarises the cell by cell differences between the model and data tables, making allowances (by means of the model's degrees of freedom) for the number of constraints imposed on the fitting of the model. A similar indicator of fit is used to assess loglinear models, although the goodness of fit statistic conventionally used is not the chi square, but a related measure called, in full, the log likelihood ratio statistic or more shortly, *G square*. The log likelihood ratio statistic is defined by:

$$G^2 = 2 \ \Sigma \ x_{ij}(\log x_{ij} - \log m_{ij})$$

where, as before, x_{ij} are the data cell frequencies, m_{ij} are the model cell frequencies, 'log' represents natural logarithm, and the summation is carried out over all the cells in the table. G square is generally calculated by the computer program used to perform iterative scaling. It has a distribution which is almost the same as the chi square statistic, and so to look up a G square probability, one can use a chi square table.

Before we can use G square to examine the fit of models, we need to know how to calculate the appropriate number of degrees of freedom. In Chapter 4 it was said that degrees of freedom are an inverse measure of the number of constraints under which the model table frequencies are calculated. The more constraints the model has to satisfy, the lower the number of degrees of freedom. When we construct loglinear models, the constraints are those marginals which are required to be identical in the model and the data. The more marginals specified in a model, therefore, the less the resulting degrees of freedom.

In fact, a model has degrees of freedom equal to the number of cells in the table minus the total number of degrees of freedom of each of its fitted marginals. Similarly, each marginal table has degrees of freedom equal to its number of cells less the total degrees of freedom of *its* marginals.

To illustrate measuring the fit of a model, let us work through the calculation of the significance figure for the no interaction model which was developed for the Banbury class by tenure by vote data (the data table of Table 5.1 and the model table of Table 5.3). Recall that we found this model gave a table which had frequencies similar but not identical to the data table. Because the two tables differed, this added credence to the Banbury study's claim that the data demonstrated statistical interaction between occupational class, type of tenure and voting behaviour. But at the time we were not able to quantify or assess the magnitude of the difference between the two tables. This we are now ready to do.

G square can be calculated (preferably using a computer) by applying the above formula to the model and data table frequencies. One finds that G square is equal to 41. The calculation of the degrees of freedom is quite straightforward, provided one takes it step by step. The model table includes five (class) by four (tenure) by two (vote) or 40 cells. The model which was fitted, written out in full to include all the lower-order relatives and abbreviating the variables for the sake of space to C, T and V, is:

$$[C,T] [C,V] [T,V] [C] [T] [V]$$

Each term in this specification represents one fitted marginal for which allowance has to be made in calculating the degrees of freedom. There is one further marginal which, in effect, has been fitted when the model table was constructed: the total number of respondents. Since the model table was calculated to include the same number of respondents as the data table, this constitutes a further constraint.

To compute the model's degrees of freedom, the degrees of freedom of each of the fitted marginals must first be found. The degrees of freedom of the 'number of respondents' marginal is one. The degrees of freedom of the class [C] marginal is equal to the number of cells in this marginal (5) minus the number of degrees of freedom of its marginals. It has only one marginal, the table total with one degree of freedom, so that its degrees of freedom is five minus one, or four (see (a) in Table 6.5). Similarly, the degrees of freedom of the marginals of tenure and vote are three and one, respectively.

The degrees of freedom of the marginal table class by tenure is equal to the number of cells in this table minus the sum of the degrees of freedom of its three marginals: the class marginal, the tenure marginal and the table total. Since the number of cells in the marginal table is twenty, its degrees of freedom is

$$20 - (4 + 3 + 1) = 12$$

(see (b) in Table 6.5). Similarly, the degrees of freedom of the marginal table class by vote is four; and of tenure by vote, three.

We are now ready to calculate the degrees of freedom of the table as a whole, and the arithmetic is shown in (c) in Table 6.5. We find that the no interaction model applied to this data has twelve degrees of freedom. Whilst it is useful to have an idea of how degrees of freedom are calculated, in practice the computer program which calculates the model table will also provide the number of degrees of freedom, so one does not normally have to work it out by hand.

Table 6.5   *Calculation of Degrees of Freedom* (df)

(a)	'Class' marginal		
	Number of cells =		5
	minus *df* of table total =		1
	Df of 'class' marginal =		4
(b)	'Class by tenure' marginal		
	Number of cells = 5 × 4 =		20
	minus *df* of 'class' marginal =	4	
	df of 'tenure' marginal =	3	
	df of table total =	1	
			8
	Df of 'class by tenure' marginal =		12
(c)	Model		
	Number of cells = 5 × 4 × 2 =		40
	minus *df* of 'class by tenure' =	12	
	df of 'class by vote' =	4	
	df of 'tenure by vote' =	3	
	df of 'class' marginal =	4	
	df of 'tenure' marginal =	3	
	df of 'vote' marginal =	1	
	df of table total =	1	
	Df of model =		28
			12

Having now both the G square value and the degrees of freedom for this model, we can turn to a table of chi square values to look up the corresponding significance level. We find that the significance is less than 0·01 per cent. A perfectly fitting model would have yielded a significance level of 100 per cent; the no interaction model we fitted has produced such a low significance level that one can reject it as inappropriate for this data without hesitation.

The reason for a model failing to fit is that in specifying it one has omitted a relationship, or some relationships, which exist in the data. However, in this case, the only relationship omitted was the interaction between the variables; all the associations have been explicitly included and all the main effects were included as lower-order relatives. Hence, we can immediately conclude that there must be interaction in the data, and that it is this which is causing the lack of fit.

Table 6.6   *Standardised Cell Residuals Obtained by Fitting a Model of 'No Interaction' to the Banbury Data in Table 5.1*

Voted Conservative

Occupational class	Own, outright	Own, on mortgage	Rented, privately	Rented, from council
		Tenure		
I and II	− 0·22	0·17	1·11	− 1·50
IIIa, IVa	− 0·36	0·17	1·11	− 1·50
IIIb	0·86	− 0·03	− 2·19	2·21
IVb	− 0·46	− 0·28	0·51	0·29
V	0·94	− 0·28	1·08	− 1·31

Voted Labour

Occupational class	Own, outright	Own, on mortgage	Rented, privately	Rented, from council
		Tenure		
I and II	0·69	− 0·34	− 1·67	2·01
IIIa, IVa	1·02	0·06	− 1·32	0·55
IIIb	− 1·11	− 0·03	1·36	− 1·22
IVb	0·61	0·25	− 0·34	− 0·17
V	− 1·30	0·25	− 0·72	0·78

One can look at the difference between the model and data tables in more detail by computing what are known as *standardised cell residuals*. Essentially, standardised residuals are the cell by cell components which are squared and summed when one calculates the chi square statistic. So the residual for cell i,j is:

$$z_{ij} = (x_{ij} - m_{ij})/\sqrt{m_{ij}}$$

Table 6.6 gives the residuals for the no interaction model.

These residuals have an approximately normal distribution with a mean of zero and a standard deviation of one, so, as a rule of thumb, those greater than 2 or less than − 2 are 'large'. There are three such large residuals in Table 6.6, each indicating a cell for which the interaction effect is particularly marked. We see that there are more skilled-manual (class IIIb) Conservative-voting council tenants and more professional and managerial (classes I and II) Labour-voting council tenants in the data table than would be expected if there were no interaction. It is, therefore, amongst these categories of people that the joint effect of class and tenure has the most influence on voting behaviour.

Table 6.7 relates respondents' attitudes towards doctors giving health advice to their sex and social class (Arber and Sawyer, 1979). We will not analyse this table by first choosing a likely model to examine, as we have done before. Instead, we shall adopt a 'brute force' approach, calculating in turn the fit of every model which could be applied to the data. This isn't an approach which one would normally advise, but it will be instructive to compare the fit of a complete range of models.

Table 6.7 *Attitudes to Doctors Giving Health Advice, by Sex and Social Class*

	Males			Females		
Class	I and II	III	IV and V	I and II	III	IV and V
Should give advice*	134	141	40	108	150	55
Only if relevant	27	47	14	47	58	19
Should not give advice	18	36	10	25	46	19

* *Question*:
  Do you feel that doctors should or should not give advice on how to keep healthy (for example, about not smoking, taking exercise and eating the right foods) whenever patients are consulting them about other things?
Source: derived from Arber and Sawyer, 1979, table 9.1.

The G square, degrees of freedom and significance of each model (specified in terms of its sufficient statistics) are shown in Table 6.8. As one moves up the table, the models include more and more relationships. The very high G square and zero significance levels of the bottom five models (14–18) show, unsurprisingly, that one needs at least one or two main effects in the model for it to fit the data even approximately. Models 10 and 11 do not fit, because they too omit the main effect of either class, or attitude. But, excepting these, one can see that as further relationships are added the fit improves, the interaction model fitting perfectly.

Which model should we adopt as the one which is the simplest that fits the data to an adequate degree? To decide, we need to adopt a standard of what is to count as an adequate fit, and the one conventionally used is that models with a significance level of 5 per cent or more are judged to fit well. Using this criterion, models 1–8 fit acceptably and model 12 just scrapes in.

It must be emphasised that the 5 per cent mark is simply a convention. There is no statistical law which requires that a model must achieve a 5 per cent significance level, if it is to fit the data. The convention is merely a convenient way of translating the verbal comment that a model fits reasonably well into a numerical score and one must, therefore, be on one's guard against reifying the convention into an absolute standard.

Table 6.8   Loglinear Models Fitted to Data on Attitudes to Doctors Giving Health Advice (Table 6.7)

Model*	G^2	Df	Significance (%)
(1) [A,C,S]	0	0	100
(2) [A,C][C,S][A,S]	4·27	4	37·1
(3) [A,C][C,S]	10·78	6	9·5
(4) [A,C][S,A]	7·49	6	27·7
(5) [C,S][S,A]	10·38	8	23·8
(6) [A,C][S]	14·43	8	7·1
(7) [C,S][A]	17·32	10	6·7
(8) [S,A][C]	14·03	10	17·1
(9) [A,C]	18·05	9	3·4
(10) [C,S]	395·11	12	0·0
(11) [S,A]	187·45	12	0·0
(12) [A][C][S]	20·99	12	5·1
(13) [A][C]	24·59	13	2·6
(14) [A][S]	194·39	14	0·0
(15) [C][S]	398·76	14	0·0
(16) [A]	198·01	15	0·0
(17) [C]	402·38	15	0·0
(18) [S]	572.18	16	0·0

* Variables abbreviated:
  A – attitude to doctors giving advice;
  C – occupational class;
  S – sex.

Of the models listed in Table 6.8, the simplest (the one involving the least relationships) which passes the 5 per cent mark is model 12, the 'no association' model. But model 8, including one association between attitude and sex, has a much better significance level and is only slightly more complex. We might, therefore, choose this one to fit the data in preference to the 'no association' model. It is of some interest that we can find an adequate model which does not include the attitude by class relationship which might have been predicted from previous work on doctors and patients. The relationship is not strong enough in the data to be needed in a good model, indicating that the association between attitudes to doctors giving health advice and social class is not as strong as one might have expected.

The Effect of the Sampling Design

One can only legitimately use G square as a measure of goodness of fit and for model selection, if the sample from which the data was obtained was randomly selected. Fortunately G square is a fairly robust measure, and most of the random sampling designs likely to be used by social researchers are quite satisfactory bases for loglinear analysis. One point must be watched, however. The sample design itself may fix certain main effects, associations, or interactions, and this must be allowed for in the interpretation of loglinear models.

For instance, the researchers who obtained the data of Table 3.2 on divorce and sexual relations deliberately included roughly equal numbers of divorced and married people in their *sample*. It would obviously not be correct to infer from the near-zero main effect for the marital status variable that there are equal numbers of married and divorced in the *population* at large. Similarly, a stratified sample in which class and sex were the stratifying variables could not be used to obtain results about the relationship between class and sex, because the association between these variables is fixed by design.

The usual practice is to include terms representing any relationships which are fixed by design in all the models one examines. This makes sure that relationships resulting solely from the sample design are taken care of by the model and can thereafter be ignored. It follows, furthermore, that one should be explicit about the sample designs one uses, so that it is clear which variables and relationships are fixed by design.

Summary

Loglinear models may be specified in terms of the marginals which are constrained to be equal in model and data tables. For three-dimensional tables, the choice of marginals includes those corresponding to main effects (for individual variables), associations and an interaction. If the latter is specified, the model will necessarily fit exactly. The fit of a model is assessed using a test of significance based on the log likelihood test statistic, or G square. The value of this statistic, in conjunction with the number of degrees of freedom of the model, is compared with the chi square distribution to establish a significance level. Models with a significance above 5 per cent are generally said to fit the data well.

We have now covered all the basic elements of loglinear analysis. Our examples have all been confined to three-dimensional tables for simplicity of exposition. However, the analysis of four and higher dimensional tables, to be demonstrated in Chapter 7, involves only a natural extension of these ideas and no new principles.

Further Reading

Bishop, Fienberg and Holland (1975, chapter 2) give proofs and further results about hierarchical models and their sufficient statistics. Atkins and Jarrett (1979) discuss more fully the limitations of the conventional approach to significance tests. Bishop, Fienberg and Holland also go into further detail about G square, and justify its use in place of chi square for loglinear analysis.

7

High-Dimension Tables

In previous chapters, we have looked at a variety of three-dimensional tables and have shown how one can develop models to fit them. The techniques we have used can be readily extended to suit tables including more variables. When analysing such complex tables, it is especially important to work one's way through the range of appropriate models in a systematic way. A technique known as forward selection can be used to guide the selection of the best model, and in this chapter we shall demonstrate forward selection on a four- and five-dimensional table. The first example will also serve as a good illustration of the comparative power of loglinear analysis for exploring tables involving more variables than can conveniently be handled by other methods, such as elaboration.

We shall look, first, at some of the factors which might influence people's ideas about how satisfactory their standard of living and financial circumstances are. Obviously, one of the most important of these is likely to be their income. But reference group theory (Merton, 1968; Runciman, 1966) suggests that people assess their standard of living not only in absolute terms, but also by comparing their situation with that of others. Hence the breadth of people's horizons, and the choices they make about whom they compare themselves with are also relevant. Furthermore, people's past experiences – in particular, their parents' standard of living and the changes in their own standard of living – may well be important. So, too, could be their level of education. All these factors could be expected to influence judgements about how satisfied one is with one's standard of living.

We can begin to explore these possibilities using data taken from the National Opinion Research Centre's General Social Survey. NORC (ICPSR, 1978) annually questions a large random sample of

US residents on a wide range of issues and makes the resulting data publicly available for further secondary analysis.

The questions include five relevant to our interests. Respondents were asked how satisfied they were about their current financial situation, and also how they thought their income compared with that of other US families. They were questioned about how their family income had compared with that of other families when they were aged 16, and whether they thought their own family circumstances had been getting better or worse during the last few years. These four questions together provide data on respondents' perceptions of their financial circumstances at present and in the past, relative to the perceived standard of living of their compatriots. We shall also use data from a question which inquired about the respondents' level of education, as measured by the number of years of school or college they had completed. All this data can be cross-classified to yield a five-dimensional table of four variables concerned with perceptions of family circumstances, and one variable indicating educational level.

This data table includes 300 cells and is too large to reproduce here. The responses from six similar surveys conducted in 1972–8 were combined, giving a total sample size of 10,307 randomly selected US citizens aged between 18 and 99. This table is the basis for the exploration of the factors affecting satisfaction with current standard of living which follows.

Our prime concern will be with the inter-relationships between the five variables just described. Of these variables, the first four are all concerned with respondents' *perceptions* of their relative income as compared with others. We shall not here be analysing the effect of their *actual* income. There is undoubtedly an association between respondents' income and their satisfaction with their financial circumstances. (Indeed, Cramer's V, a measure of strength of relationship similar to phi, but appropriate for tables with more than two levels per variable, is equal to 0.21 for the association between income and satisfaction with current income.) However, this is incidental to the focus of this example, which is concerned more with the relationships between various perceptions and changes in perceptions about income.

Analysing a five-dimensional table is much the same as analysing smaller ones. One difference lies in the range of components that are available to build models. With the three-dimensional tables we have encountered so far, there has only been one possible interaction effect, the one representing the interaction between the three variables. In five-dimensional tables one can have interactions occurring between any combination of three of the five variables. There can, therefore, be ten different interactions. Moreover, with five variables, higher-order effects are also possible. Thus, one may find effects (known as *second-order interactions*) representing the difference in the interaction between three variables for the various levels of a fourth variable. (Compare the definition of an interaction as the difference in association between two variables for various levels of a third.) Finally, a third-order interaction may exist, when a second-order interaction differs according to the levels of a fifth variable. Fortunately for one's sanity, second- and third-order interactions are rarely found in practice; on the occasions when they are, they are often singularly difficult to interpret in readily comprehensible sociological terms.

Returning to our example, although the discussion about reference groups, above, indicated that there are quite likely to be associations between most of the five variables and that there may even be interactions amongst them, it is not immediately clear which particular model we should choose to examine first. Our theoretical preconceptions are not sufficiently precise to justify the selection of one specific set of inter-relationships as an initial model. This is frequently the case when one is dealing with real research problems, and is the reason for engaging in exploratory data analysis. Because we don't know much about the likely structure in the data, we shall use a model selection procedure known as *forward selection*.

Forward selection involves first examining the very simplest model for its fit, and then successively adding further effects until sufficient have been included for the fit to be good. The simplest model which can be fitted to a data table is the *grand mean* model, one that has not previously been described. It is a model in which all the cell frequencies are exactly the same, so that respondents are distributed uniformly through the table. Such a model table is, of course, highly unlikely to be a good fit in any data table encountered in practice. The grand mean model is, therefore, rarely proposed as a model to fit real data. Nevertheless, it does serve a useful purpose as a point of comparison or 'benchmark' in terms of which the fit of more complex models may be assessed, because it will always be the worst-fitting of any we care to try. The grand mean model is straightforward to calculate: one simply divides the total number of respondents by the number of cells, and puts the resulting frequency into each cell of the table.

The first step of forward selection is, therefore, to fit the grand mean model (see Table 7.1). Having found, without surprise, that it does not fit, we try a main effects model in which is included each of the single-variable marginals (Table 7.1, model 2). This model does not fit well either, so we move to a pairwise association model (model 3) and then to a model including all possible sets of

Table 7.1 Models Fitted to Data on Perceptions of Satisfaction with Financial Circumstances

	Model*	G^2	Df	Significance (%)
(1)	Grand mean	26,235	299	0
(2)	[S][F][I][A][E]	5,331	287	0
(3)	[S,F][S,I][S,A][S,E][F,I]	280	234	2
	[F,A][F,E][I,A][I,E][A,E]			
(4)	[S,F,I][S,F,A][F,I,A][S,F,E]			
	[F,A,E][S,I,E][F,I,E][S,A,E][I,A,E]	111	123	78
(5)	Pairwise associations (model 3)			
(5.1)	plus [S,F,I]	263	218	2
(5.2)	plus [S,F,A]	259	226	6
(5.3)	plus [S,I,A]	267	226	3
(5.4)	plus [F,I,A]	246	202	2
(5.5)	plus [S,F,E]	244	230	26
(5.6)	plus [F,A,E]	254	226	9
(5.7)	plus [S,I,E]	275	230	2
(5.8)	plus [F,I,E]	255	213	2
(5.9)	plus [S,A,E]	276	232	3
(5.10)	plus [I,A,E]	269	226	3
(6)	[S,F,E][S,I][F,I][S,A][F,A][I,A][I,E][A,E] (model 5.5)			
(6.1)	minus [S,I]	256	234	16
(6.2)	minus [F,I]	787	246	0
(6.3)	minus [S,A]	847	232	0
(6.4)	minus [F,A]	1,096	238	0
(6.5)	minus [I,A]	254	238	22
(6.6)	minus [I,E]	627	234	0
(6.7)	minus [A,E]	411	232	0
(7)	[S,F,E][F,I][S,A][F,A][I,E][A,E]	266	242	14

* Model abbreviations:

S – satisfaction with current financial circumstances;

F – how family income compares with that of US families in general;

I – how family income when aged 16 compares with that of other US families at that time;

A – whether financial circumstances have improved or got worse in recent years;

E – level of education.

interactions (model 4). At last we have a model which fits well, as shown by its significance level of 78 per cent.

However, in reaching this model, we have jumped from all associations to *all* interactions, neglecting to examine intermediate models including only one or a few interactions; although such simpler models might also fit quite adequately. The next step in the forward selection procedure is, therefore, to see whether all the interaction terms in the model are really necessary. This is done by reverting to the pairwise association model and finding the fit when just one of the interactions is added, for each interaction in turn.

Models 5.1–5.9 show the results: all the 'association plus one interaction' models have a significance level below 5 per cent, except models 5.5 and 5.6. Noting that model 5.5 has the highest significance level (26 per cent), we can conclude that all the interactions other than [S,F,E] can be pulled out of model 4 (giving model 6) without destroying the fit.

Model 6 is clearly much simpler than model 4, since it includes one rather than ten interactions. But it may still be possible to simplify it further by removing unnecessary associations. Because we are only using hierarchical models, the associations which are lower-order relatives of [S,F,E], that is [S,F], S,E] and [F,E], cannot be deleted. All the other associations are candidates for removal, and models 6.1–6.7 show the consequences of taking each of them, one at a time, out of model 6. Removing both [S,I] and [I,A] individually, leaves a model with a significance level well over 5 per cent; it seems that neither association is necessary in the model. Model 7 is, then, the one that results from taking both these associations out of model 6, and is the final model obtained by forward selection.

To summarise what we have done, forward selection involves the following steps:

(1) Try models including all 'level *L*' effects successively, for '*L*' equal to zero (that is, the grand mean model), equal to one (main effects), equal to two (associations), and so on, until a model is found which fits.

(2) Return to the model before the one which fitted (that is, return to the level *L* − 1 model). Examine all models including any one level *L* effect; if none fit, examine those including any two level *L* effects, and so on, until a model is found which fits. (In the example above, a model was found which fitted after examining those including just one level *L* effect, but in other

cases one may not be so lucky, requiring for example a model including two interactions.)

(3) Remove the $L - 1$ level effects one at a time, until no more may be deleted without reducing the fit to an unacceptable degree.

The simplest model which fits the data obtained by forward selection is:

$$[S,F,E] \, [F,I] \, [S,A] \, [F,A] \, [I,E] \, [A,E]$$

What can one infer from this?

First, the model confirms that many of the indicators of perceptions of past and present financial circumstances are associated, as we had initially supposed. In particular, respondents' views on how their parents' family incomes compared with those of other families are related to their views about their circumstances relative to other families now. Their educational level is related to their views on how well off their parents were, perhaps because there is a tendency for the sons and daughters of rich parents to stay in education for longer than the poor. The respondents' assessments about whether their circumstances have got better or worse over the last few years are related to their educational level, their current satisfaction with their finances and with their ideas about how their current circumstances compare with that of other families. The interaction term in the model indicates that the relationship between respondents' views on how satisfied they are with their income and their ideas on how that income compares with that of other families varies with their level of education. This can easily be explained using the notion that education tends to broaden people's horizons, so that the better educated are likely to compare their incomes not just with a small circle of people known to them but with a much wider spread of people.

The forward selection method is a convenient technique for sifting through a very great number of models to find one which is both relatively simple, and which fits adequately. It is not, however, without its weaknesses. First, some models are never examined if one follows the method. For instance, a model including a pair of interactions and no associations, other than lower-order relatives, might turn out to be a better model than the one which we selected; we do not know because no models of this type were explored. Secondly, on some occasions the method yields not one, but two alternative models. For instance in the example, model 5.6 fits with a significance level of 9 per cent. We could have examined this model further, rather than choosing model 5.5. We might well have finished with a model not much more complex than model 7, which fitted the data just about as well, but which included a different interaction term. Forward selection has nothing to say about choosing between such alternative models. Such decisions have to be made using one's sociological knowledge about what sort of model seems most plausible. Thirdly, forward selection is a purely mechanical procedure, which leaves no room for prior ideas and the analyst's goals to enter directly into the choice of a model. Nevertheless, despite these problems, it seems in practice to locate a reasonable model in most cases.

Although model 7 of Table 7.1 is the best model forward selection can find, this does not mean that the model is necessarily particularly good at explaining the data. It would be useful to know also just how good this 'best' model is. There are, however, two quite different criteria we could use in assessing the model. On the one hand, we could be interested in how well the data cell frequencies are fitted by the model. We shall shortly introduce a measure which will allow this to be quantified, and in fact we shall find that the model we have chosen fits the data cell frequencies very well. On the other hand, we could be interested in how completely the model explains people's level of satisfaction with their financial circumstances. This is really a question about whether all the relevant variables have been included in the model. Since only variables occurring in the data table were tried in the model, we must also ask whether all relevant variables have been included in the data table.

The answer to this latter question must be no. As was noted above, the level of respondents' actual income is an important determinant of level of satisfaction, and there are many other variables which could also be influential. In short, the data table we have been using tells some, but by no means all, of the story about levels of satisfaction. The part of the story it does tell is represented by the associations and interaction in the model we have fitted. However, *no* statistical measure based on that data table will help us decide how much of the complete explanation of satisfaction we have found. No measure will indicate whether we have included five relatively important or five relatively trivial variables in constructing the table. This means that the part of the story told by the variables we have omitted from the table may, in fact, be much more interesting and significant than the part we have found, but we have no way of telling whether this is so.

It is therefore incumbent on the researcher to ensure that those variables which he thinks will be important are included in his data table, and to justify the exclusion of other variables. This can only be done by recourse to the theoretical framework which underlies the research he is doing. With this in mind, we can now see how well the model we have selected fits the data we have got. Remembering that a zero value of G square indicates that the data has been fitted perfectly, it is reasonable to interpret a non-zero value of G square as indicating the amount of variation in the data cell frequencies left unexplained by a model. A model which gives a fit with a G square value of zero explains all the variation in the data; a model with a large value of G square explains relatively little. This idea is exploited in defining the *coefficient of multiple determination*, which measures the proportion of the total variation in data cell frequencies explained by a model.

The coefficient is calculated by comparing the relative fit of the selected model with the fit of a 'minimal' model including no effects, that is, with the grand mean model. Thus, the coefficient of multiple determination for our selected model, which has a G square value of 266, is:

$$(G^2_{\text{grand mean}} - G^2_{\text{model 7}}) / G^2_{\text{grand mean}}$$

$$= \quad (26{,}235 - 266)/26{,}235$$

$$= \quad 0 \cdot 99$$

meaning that the model has explained 99 per cent of the variation in the data table.

To conclude this chapter, let us look at another table using forward selection. Table 7.2 displays data from a well-known study by Stouffer *et al.* (1949), about the preference of Second World War recruits for the location of their training-camp. Table 7.3 summarises the results of forward selection. Note that models including only one interaction term seem to be insufficient to fit this data, since all such models failed to give a significance level above 5 per cent. Hence, it was necessary to move to a model including two interactions. The only association which is not a lower-order relative of the best two-interaction model could not be deleted without

Table 7.2   *Preference of Second World War Recruits for the Location of their Training-Camp*

Race (R)	Region of origin (O)	Location of present camp (L)	Number of recruits (P) preferring a camp	
			in north	*in south*
Black	North	North	387	36
		South	876	250
	South	North	383	270
		South	381	1,712
White	North	North	955	162
		South	874	510
	South	North	104	176
		South	91	869

Source: adapted from Stouffer *et al.*, 1949, with those undecided omitted.

destroying the fit. (Make sure that you follow the logic of the choice of models to test shown in Table 7.3; it is one of the most complex you are likely to encounter.)

The final model shows that preference for location of training-camp (variable *P*) depends on race (*R*), region of origin (*O*), location of present camp (*L*) and the interaction between region of origin and location of present camp. The latter assertion amounts to saying that the preferred location depends on where the respondent is at present, but the strength of this relationship varies according to his original place of residence. Moreover, there is an interaction between present location, race and region of origin, that is, the location of the respondent varies according to his region of origin, but more or less strongly depending on the respondent's race. We might suspect that the influence of race on the association between region of origin and present location may be a sign of racial discrimination in the allocation of recruits to training-camps.

In this chapter we have shown how one can find a model to fit a complex table. The models which were chosen using forward selection involved both associations and interactions. The next question one is likely to ask is whether all the relationships in a model are equally important. It may be that one or more of them are very weak, having little substantive significance. What we need, therefore, is a way of measuring the strengths of effects. In Chapter 4 we discussed measuring the strength of an association in a two-dimensional table; in Chapter 8 we review the measures which can be used for more complex tables.

Table 7.3   *Forward Selection on the Data of Table 7.2*

Model*	G^2	Df	Significance (%)
Grand mean	5,470	15	0
[P][L][O][R]	4,211	11	0
[P,L][P,O][P,R][L,O][L,R][O,R]	78	5	0
[P,L,O][P,L,R][P,O,R][L,O,R]	1	1	58
[P,L,O][P,R][L,R][O,R]	46	4	0
[P,L,R][P,O][L,O][O,R]	77	4	0
[P,O,R][P,L][L,O][L,R]	73	4	0
[L,O,R][P,L][P,O][P,R]	25	4	0
[P,L,O][P,L,R][O,R]	34	3	0
[P,L,O][P,O,R][L,R]	36	3	0
[P,L,O][L,O,R][P,R]	2	3	70
[P,L,R][P,O,R][L,O]	72	3	0
[P,L,R][L,O,R][P,O]	17	3	0
[P,O,R][L,O,R][P,L]	25	3	0
[P,L,O][L,O,R]	153	4	0
Model selected: [P,L,O][L,O,R][P,R]	2	3	70

* *Variable abbreviations:*

  P – preferred location of camp;

  L – present location of camp;

  O – region of origin;

  R – race.

Summary

Although the analysis of higher-dimension tables is similar to that of tables involving only three variables, the added dimensions do introduce two complications. First, second- and third-order interactions may be found, although in practice these occur infrequently. Secondly, a great number of models may be fitted to such tables, making a strategy for finding the best necessary. One such strategy, forward selection, will usually reveal the best-fitting model fairly quickly. Nevertheless, it must be remembered that the 'best' model may actually fit the data rather poorly.

Further Reading

Bishop, Fienberg and Holland (1975) deal with a variety of methods of model choice, including forward selection and backward elimination, and discuss their relative merits. See also Benedetti and Brown (1978). Davis (1973) offers an example of forward selection. The coefficient of multiple determination was introduced by Goodman (1972a).

8

The Strength of
Loglinear Effects

In Chapter 7, we identified the simplest model which fitted data on satisfaction with one's standard of living. This model had six terms, each of which was shown to be significant in the sense that removing any of them led to a model which no longer fitted, using the 5 per cent criterion level. However, the fact that each of the six effects was needed in the model does not mean that they all represent substantively important relationships. It may be that particular terms correspond to relationships which, although present in the data, are nevertheless so small in magnitude that they can be neglected as trivial in any sociological analysis. In order to see whether this is so, one needs to be able to assess the magnitude of a relationship, and it is with this problem that this chapter is concerned.

Table 8.1   *Belief in a Deity by Sex: Invented Data from 200 Respondents*

	Sex	
	Male	*Female*
Believes in existence of deity	40	41
Does not believe in deity	60	59

The distinction between a statistically significant and a substantively significant effect is an important one. Let us suppose that in some population 40 per cent of males believe in the existence of a deity and 41 per cent of females do so. Clearly, the relationship between this religious belief and sex is of no sociological importance whatever: no social researcher would worry about explaining such a very small difference between men and women. Table 8.1 shows the results one might get from a survey of 100 males and 100 females drawn from this population. Fitting a model of no association to the table yields a G square of 0·02 which, with one degree of freedom, gives a significance level of 88 per cent – no association between the variables has been detected. Now consider Table 8.2, showing the results from a much more ambitious survey of 200,000 individuals. Although the table is based on exactly the same population, again with 40 and 41 per cent of males and females stating that they believe in a deity, fitting a model of no association gives a G square equal to $20 \cdot 7$ and a significance level of $0 \cdot 01$ per cent, showing that there is association in this table.

Table 8.2   *Belief in a Deity by Sex: Invented Data from 200,000 Respondents*

	Sex	
	Male	*Female*
Believes in existence of deity	40,000	41,000
Does not believe in deity	60,000	59,000

The moral to be drawn from this illustration is that the power of loglinear analysis to detect a relationship depends not only on its strength, but also on the sample size. Given a large enough sample, even entirely trivial effects may be detected. Conversely, the fact that an effect must be included in a model in order for the model to fit adequately does not mean that the effect is of any practical importance; it may be quite insubstantial. More than knowledge of significance levels is needed to measure the strengths of relationships.

It is necessary to be very clear on this point, because both the measures of significance with which we have so far been concerned and the measures of the strengths of relationship to be introduced below are functions of G square, and so it is easy to get confused over what one is measuring. The same confusion can and sometimes does arise when using the traditional measures of significance and strength of relationship in simple two-dimensional tables. Novice researchers sometimes mistakenly use chi square, a measure of significance, to assess the strength of a relationship when they should be using a measure of association such as phi.

As we saw in the illustration above, enlarging the sample size will affect the value of measures of significance, because they are dependent on the absolute magnitude of differences in frequencies within a data table. Measures of association are not sensitive to the actual magnitude of the data frequencies, but depend on the proportions of the sample which fall into each cell. Changing the sample size should, therefore, have no effect on measures of association.

The principle employed to assess the strength of a relationship in the context of loglinear analysis can be simply stated: one contrasts the fit of two models, one including the effect in which one is interested, and the other excluding it. The strength of the relationship is a function of the difference in the fit of these two models. This procedure works because if a relationship is weak, it will have little influence on the distribution of cell frequencies in the data table. Hence, excluding the corresponding term from a model will make little difference to that model's fit with the data. On the other hand, if the relationship is strong, tables derived from models with and without the effect will be very different and the model including the effect will fit much better than the one without it.

However, before one can apply this principle, two issues have to be settled:

(1) which particular pair of models are to be contrasted;
(2) how the difference in their fits is to be assessed.

There are usually a large number of models available which differ only by one effect. Since it is already familiar, let us use the example discussed in Chapter 7, and examine the strength of the association between respondents' perceptions of their comparative financial circumstances when interviewed and when aged 16. Using the abbreviations for the variables listed in Table 7.1, Table 8.3 shows just a few of the pairs of models which differ only by the term relating to this association ($[F,I]$). There are many more such pairs, including those involving other interaction effects and other combinations of associations. The large number of pairs of models which could be contrasted would not matter if they yielded the same result for the strength of the relationship, but they do not.

The values of the strength of the association $[F,I]$ obtained from contrasting these pairs of models differ, because in each case one is controlling for the additional effects included in the models. To explain the consequences of this, consider the first and last of the pairs listed. The first includes all the other effects which we found to be significant when modelling the data in Chapter 7. Thus the difference between the fit of the first pair of models is the result of removing the $[F,I]$ effect, taking into account (by including in the models) all the other significant relationships. Another way of

Table 8.3   *A Few of the Pairs of Models which Differ Only by the Term Representing the Association between Perceptions of Current and Past Financial Circumstances Relative to that of Other Families*

(1a)	[S,F,E]	[F,I]	[S,A]	[F,A]	[I,E]	[A,E]		
(1b)	[S,F,E]		[S,A]	[F,A]	[I,E]	[A,E]		
(2a)		[F,I]	[S,A]	[F,A]	[I,E]	[A,E]		
(2b)			[S,A]	[F,A]	[I,E]	[A,E]		
(3a)		[F,I]		[F,A]	[I,E]	[A,E]	[S]	
(3b)				[F,A]	[I,E]	[A,E]	[S]	
(4a)		[F,I]			[I,E]	[A,E]	[S]	
(4b)					[I,E]	[A,E]	[S]	
(5a)		[F,I]				[A,E]	[S]	
(5b)						[A,E]	[S]	[F]	[I]
(6a)		[F,I]						
(6b)								[F]	[I]

Note:
Variables abbreviated as in Table 7.1.

describing the difference is that it is the result of the association between the two variables, controlling for other relationships. The relationship one measures by contrasting this pair of models is known as the *partial* relationship; it is a generalisation to multidimensional tables of the partial association described in Chapter 4.

The last pair of models (6a and 6b) omit all effects other than [F,I]. Model 6a consists only of this term, 6b is derived from 6a by removing the association term, but leaving its lower-order relatives, the two main effects. Contrasting these two models, yields a measure of the association between the variables equal to the association one would have found, if one knew nothing of the influence of the other variables; as would have been the case, if the survey from which the data was derived had been limited solely to measuring these two variables and no others. Again by considering the simple case of a three-dimensional table, one can see that contrasting this pair of models yields a measure of the *marginal* relationship.

The other pairs listed in Table 8.3 would give values of the strength of the association controlling for some but not all of the other relationships in the data; the results are not as easily interpretable as the partial and marginal ones. Partial and marginal measures can be calculated for any effect by choosing appropriate pairs of models, although the two measures are identical for main effects. Generally one finds that the partial relationship is weaker than the marginal one. This is because the partial relationship is the 'pure', intrinsic relationship between the two variables. The marginal relationship includes both the partial relationship, and the contributions from the chains of relationship linking the two variables via other variables in the table.

Table 8.4 provides an illustration of this point. The table displays data about reading habits, cross-tabulating the number of books the respondent claims to have read in the previous year by age and education. We can find the cross-product ratio (as a simple and familiar measure of the strength of association) for each of the two partial tables of reading by age, controlling for education. The ratios for the partial tables are both near one, indicating little association between reading and age amongst those with the same level of education. However, the cross-product ratio for the marginal table obtained by summing over the categories of education is 1·64, showing that the marginal association is of moderate strength.

There is a marginal association between age and reading, despite the very low partial association, because each of the variables age and reading are separately associated with education (the cross-product ratio for the marginal table, age by education, is 4·28 and for reading by education is 7·31). One can think of it in this way: the

Table 8.4   *Book Reading amongst a sample of Baltimore Women, by Age and Education*

(a) *Full data table*				
Education	High school		Less than High school	
Age	45 and older	Under 45	45 and older	Under 45
Reading				
Low	215	373	335	133
High	263	453	54	24

Cross-product ratios of partial tables of reading by age, controlling for education:
High school: 0·99   Less than High school: 1·11

(b) *Marginal table of reading by age*		
Age	45 and older	Under 45
Reading		
Low	550	506
High	317	477

Cross-product ratio of marginal table of reading by age: 1·64

Source: survey by J. Hajda, reported in Davis, 1971, table 4.2.

respondents' ages influence their educational level (the younger respondents being the better educated), and their educational level influences their reading habits. So, overall, the younger respondents read more. But, amongst those with little education, age makes only a slight difference to the amount they read, and similarly for the older people. Thus, the apparent (marginal) association between reading and age comes mainly from the consequences of the chains of relationship between reading and education, and age and education and not from the direct (partial) association between reading and age.

We have discussed the choice of models to contrast in order to measure the strength of a relationship; we must now move on to consider how the relative fits of these models are to be transformed into a suitable coefficient. Since the fit of a model is summarised by the value of G square obtained from comparing the model table with the data table, we can use the G squares of the pair of models as the basis for such a coefficient. So that we may describe the formulae generally, we shall henceforth use the notation G^2_I and G^2_E to mean the values of G square obtained from fitting the model *including* the effect to be measured and obtained from the model *excluding* the effect, respectively.

The simplest way to measure the difference in fit resulting from removing an effect is to subtract G^2_I from G^2_E. Note that the G square of the model excluding the effect will always be greater than or equal to the G square of the model including it, since the former will not fit as well as the latter, having fewer terms. Hence, the result of the subtraction will always be positive. However, it will have no definable maximum value. Since measures of strength of relationships are conventionally designed to take values between one and zero, the difference between G_E and G_I is divided by the G square of the model with the effect excluded, giving a measure known as the *coefficient of determination*:

$$C = (G^2_E - G^2_I) \,/\, G^2_E$$

This coefficient, therefore, measures the proportional reduction in fit consequent on the removal of an effect from a model.

The coefficient of determination has been used by Cohen and Kleugel (1978) to assess the determinants of sentencing in juvenile courts. They collected data on six variables thought to influence the severity of the sentences given in 6,894 cases of male juvenile

Table 8.5 *Models Fitted to Data on the Determinants of Disposition amongst US Juveniles Sentenced in Two Metropolitan Courts*

	Model	G^2	Df	Significance (%)
(1)	Pairwise associations	1,558	649	0·0
(2)	All interactions	419	501	99·7
(3)	Model 1 plus [I,A,R][I,R,C][A,P,D] [A,O,R][P,O,C][R,O,C] [I,R,C][O,P,D][O,C,D] (best model)	641	607	16·3
(4)	Model 3 minus [O,P,D]	727	615	0·1
(5)	Model 3 minus [O,C,D]	767	615	0·0
(6)	Model 3 minus [A,P,D]	692	609	1·0
(7)	Model 1 minus [C,D]	1,672	651	0·0
(8)	Model 1 minus [R,D]	1,559	651	0·0
(9)	Model 1 minus [O,D]	2,093	657	0·0
(10)	Model 1 minus [P,D]	1,742	651	0·0
(11)	Model 1 minus [A,D]	1,612	651	0·0
(12)	Model 1 minus [I,D]	1,568	653	0·0

Abbreviations:
   R – race;
   I – income;
   C – location of court;
   A – present activity (working, at school/idle);
   P – prior record;
   O – type of offence;
   D – severity of disposition.
Source: Cohen and Kleugel, 1978, tables 1 and 2.

delinquency heard in US courts in Denver and Memphis. The six variables which were cross-tabulated with severity of disposition were race, parental income, location of court, whether the child is either working or at school, or is 'idle', prior record, and type of offence. Table 8.5 shows some models fitted to this data, model 3 being the one judged to be the best. Table 8.6, also taken from Cohen and Kleugel, lists the coefficients of determination for each of the effects which figure in the best model and which involve severity of disposition.

The associations shown are all lower-order relatives of the terms in the model, and so their strengths could not be found by the usual device of excluding just one effect from the best-fitting model (removing a lower-order relative makes no difference to a hierarchical model, because the higher-order term necessarily still retains the effect). Hence, the lower-order associations were assessed by reference to a pairwise association model (model 1), rather than the best-fitting (model 3). Although there is no better method, the results of measuring the strengths of an effect with respect to an ill-fitting model may not be reliable, because one has ignored the consequences of some significant effects.

Table 8.6   Strengths of Effects in the Model Fitted to Data on Severity of Disposition amongst US Juveniles Sentenced in Two Metropolitan Courts

Effect	From comparison of models	Coefficient of determination (%)
[O,P,D]	4 + 3	11·9
[O,C,D]	5 + 3	18·0
[A,P,D]	6 + 3	7·7
[C,D]	7 + 1	7·0
[R,D]	8 + 1	0·2
[O,D]	9 + 1	32·7
[P,D]	10 + 1	11·5
[A,D]	11 + 1	3·1
[I,D]	12 + 1	0·6

Source: Cohen and Kleugel, 1978, table 3.

Looking at Table 8.6, we can see that the two variables with the strongest impact on severity of disposition are the type of offence committed and the juvenile's prior record. Both the association and the interaction terms involving severity of disposition by offence type and by prior record have relatively high values of the coefficient. The partial associations, severity of disposition by race and by income, have very small contributions to make, an observation which Cohen and Kleugel interpret as evidence that these courts are not biased with respect to race or social class in making judgements.

Although the coefficient of determination is quite useful for comparing the relative strengths of effects in a model, it does suffer from some limitations. For instance, it is difficult to compare the magnitude of relationships measured from different data tables. A value of the coefficient of 60 per cent may represent a substantial relationship in one table, but a minor one in another. It would obviously be better to have a measure whose values could be compared freely, and for which a particular value would always have the same meaning.

Even more important, it is highly desirable for a coefficient to have the same value irrespective of the number of variables cross-classified in the data table. For instance, in Table 8.4, one would hope that the coefficient for the *marginal* association of reading by age when measured from the full three-dimensional table would have the same value as it has when measured from the marginal table of reading by age obtained by summing over education. Unfortunately, the coefficient of determination does not have this property.

One measure which does have these desirable features is the uncertainty coefficient, which we met in Chapter 4 when applied to measuring association in two-dimensional tables. Like the coefficient of determination, the uncertainty coefficient can be expressed in terms of the proportional reduction in fit between two models, but the formula also includes a norming factor which allows for the dimensionality of the table, and an additional term in the denominator which compensates for variations in the grand mean. The uncertainty coefficient, expressed now in its general form for tables of any dimensionality, is given by:

$$U = s(G^2_E - G^2_I) / (G^2_E + D)$$

where s is the number of dimensions (variables) in the complete table, and

$$D = 2 \Sigma \; x_{ijkl}(\log x_{++++} - \log x_{ijkl})$$

(or a similar expression with the appropriate number of subscripts to suit the dimensionality of the table). Recall that i, j, k and l are subscripts indicating categories of each of the variables (you may want to refer back to Chapter 3 to refresh your memory about these). The coefficient has a range from zero to one, covering the range from no relationship to a 'perfect' relationship.

We can use the coefficient to measure the strengths of the effects we found were significant in the table on perceptions of financial circumstances. The value of the coefficient for each significant effect is shown in Table 8.7, with the coefficient of determination listed alongside for comparison. The partial coefficients were calculated using the model developed in Chapter 7 as the base (that is, as the model giving G^2_I) from which each effect in turn was deleted (to give G^2_E).

None of the associations we found are very strong. Their apparently very modest magnitude is unduly emphasised by the fact that the uncertainty coefficient tends to have a lower value, for a given association, than other similar measures. This is not a fault (its actual value, so long as it is consistent from table to table, does not matter), but it does mean that a value as low as 0·02 still represents some effect. The square root of the uncertainty coefficient has the advantage over the coefficient itself that (for associations) it usually has much the same magnitude as the values of phi and Cramer's V, the two measures of association most commonly found in the literature, and most familiar to social researchers. Table 8.7, therefore, shows the square roots in the third column.

Table 8.7   *Strengths of Effects in the Model to Fit Data on Satisfaction with Financial Circumstances*

	Effect	*Coefficient of determination*	*Uncertainty coefficient (U)*	$\sqrt{U}$
[S,F,E]	partial	0·122	0·002	0·04
	marginal	0·002	0·002	0·04
[F,I]	partial	0·704	0·034	0·19
	marginal	0·100	0·042	0·20
[S,A]	partial	0·694	0·033	0·18
	marginal	0·041	0·043	0·21
[F,A]	partial	0·769	0·048	0·22
	marginal	0·091	0·069	0·26
[I,E]	partial	0·589	0·021	0·14
	marginal	0·347	0·027	0·16
[A,E]	partial	0·391	0·009	0·10
	marginal	0·014	0·015	0·12

Note:
Abbreviations of variables as in Table 7.1.

Of the five association terms, the association between educational level and recent changes in family income is the weakest, the others being very similar. The interaction effect is likewise only of moderate strength. These results tend to confirm our earlier suspicions that we isolated only a few of the determinants of satisfaction with family income in our analysis.

Screening

Approximate values for the strengths of effects can be used as a preliminary guide to finding a good model. One can calculate the marginal and partial effects of all possible terms, and then try a model which includes only the ones with reasonably high coefficients of determination. This initial guess can then be refined to yield the best-fitting model. As we noted above, marginal and partial coefficients should be calculated using the best-fitting model as a base, and of course, this cannot be done until one knows what that model is. Nevertheless, using a pairwise association model as a base for computing coefficients for association terms, or an all-interaction model for interaction terms, one can often get reasonable approximations to the strengths of effects. This procedure, known as *screening* (Brown, 1976), can be automated, using a computer program which calculates all the coefficients. One then scans down the list, and includes in one's model those with a coefficient of determination larger than, say, 10 per cent, or an uncertainty coefficient larger than about 0·01. Screening cannot guarantee the selection of the best model immediately, in part because the coefficients are not calculated with respect to a well-fitting model, but it often does quite a good job.

Summary

Some relationships which are statistically significant, and which therefore must be included in a well-fitting model, may be very weak and of little practical significance. Such trivial effects are especially likely to be found in data from large samples. To measure the strength of a relationship, one compares the fit of a model including it, with the fit of one excluding it, the difference in fit being due to the consequences of that relationship. By choosing appropriate pairs of models to compare, one can find the strengths of partial and marginal effects, and these may be expressed in terms of the coefficient of determination or the uncertainty coefficient.

Further Reading

Measuring the strength of effects is a relatively neglected issue in the literature of loglinear analysis. The approach discussed here is based on Goodman's coefficient of partial determination (Goodman,

1972a). The u coefficient (discussed in Chapter 11) is sometimes used as a measure of the strength of an effect, but it has several serious disadvantages; Payne (1977) illustrates the uses of the u coefficient.

9

Causal Analysis

Whilst discussing the interpretation of results of loglinear analysis in previous chapters, we have occasionally made assumptions about the causal ordering of the variables we were concerned with. For example, when we discussed the data on reading habits in Chapter 8 (see Table 8.4), we found an association between respondents' educational level and the amount of reading they did. We went on to assume that this relationship was due to the causal influence of education on reading habits; that is, that the respondents who read a lot did so because they had had relatively more education (Figure 9.1). We could have made other assumptions which are equally consistent with the finding that the two variables are associated: either that reading habits causally influenced level of education, or that there is no *causal* relationship between the two. However, the first of these is very implausible – it is difficult to see how someone's education completed years previously could be affected by current reading habits. The second, that there is no causal relationship, is possible, but it then becomes difficult to imagine why we should find an association between these variables.

It is important to see that the result of the statistical analysis (that there is an association) does not itself provide any evidence to prove the existence or the direction of causality. It cannot help us to discover which variables are 'causes' and which 'effects'. Causal statements may be justified using one's common knowledge of the world, the temporal ordering of events, the results of experiments, or through theorising, but they cannot be derived solely from statistics.

The starting-point for a causal analysis must therefore be a specification of the causal ordering of the variables, showing which are assumed to have causal consequences for which. A convenient way of summarising and presenting such a specification is a causal diagram. This is a diagram in which arrows point from the assumed

Figure 9.1   *Causal diagram, showing hypothesised causal relationships between age, educational level and amount of reading.*

causal variables to the assumed affected variables. A causal diagram for the reading data is shown in Figure 9.1, and a rather more complicated example (based on the model used in Blau and Duncan's (1967) research on the American occupational structure) is shown in Figure 9.2. In both these diagrams, the antecedent, causally prior variables are on the left and those which are affected by these causes are on the right, so that the arrows tend to go from left to right. The curved, double-headed arrow in Figure 9.2 indicates an assumed association between father's education and status for which no particular statement about the direction of causality is being made. The variables to the left in the diagrams are often known as *predictor* variables, because we can use them to predict the values taken by the variables on the right. Thus the second model assumes that given a father's score on the status and education variables, we should be able to predict his son's score on the variable respondent's education.

Ordinary ideas of causality prohibit an event causing another which has already occurred. Therefore if there is a temporal order amongst the variables, our causal model must be chosen to follow

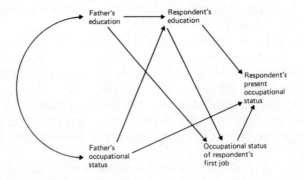

Figure 9.2   *Causal diagram, showing hypothesised causal relationships between fathers' and sons' education and income (derived from Blau and Duncan, 1967, p. 170).*

this order. Because the variables in the second diagram do have a clear order in time, sorting out which variables are predictors, and which consequences, is easy. The father variables must be predictors of the respondent variables, and respondent's education must be a predictor of respondent's present status.

In other cases, making sensible assumptions about causal ordering is very much more difficult. The difficulties may arise because we just do not have a clear idea about which variables are causes and which effects. Or the difficulties may stem from the feeling that the causation is not unidirectional: *A* causes *B*, but *B* also causes *A*. For instance, Duncan, Haller and Portes (1968) have called attention to the way in which one's peers influence one's aspirations and ambitions. They suggest that the relationship must be reciprocal – if my best friend influences my aspirations, I must also influence his. A causal arrow connecting the variables, respondent's aspiration and best friend's aspiration, should therefore be double-headed, indicating bidirectional causality (Figure 9.3). (Note that the conventional, straight double-headed arrow should be distinguished

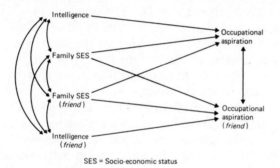

SES = Socio-economic status

Figure 9.3   *A recursive causal diagram to explain occupational aspiration (adapted from Duncan et al., 1968).*

from the curved double-headed arrow connecting father's education and income, in Figure 9.2, the latter being intended to represent a relationship for which the causal direction is for the moment undefined.)

Models in which only unidirectional causal influences are included are known as *recursive*, those with at least one reciprocal causal influence, *non-recursive*; the latter are much more difficult to deal with than the former. Some progress has been made with the analysis of non-recursive models, using methods based on the multiple regression of interval level variables (Goldberger and Duncan, 1973), but there are still major unresolved problems with the analysis of non-recursive models based on categorical data, and so here we shall only deal with the recursive variety. Indeed, even methods of analysing recursive models have not yet been developed to the point where they can answer all the questions we might want to ask. One area in which complications can arise in dealing with recursive models is the treatment and representation of interaction. The arrows between the variables in the causal models shown in Figures 9.1 and 9.2 are intended to convey that there are associations between the variables, and that these associations are the result of a causal relationship. But once we introduce interaction between three (or more) variables, a clear representation becomes more difficult. There is also some difficulty about the causal interpretation of interaction. As we noted in Chapter 4, an interaction may be described in any of three equivalent ways: as the association between A and B varying according to the levels of C; as the association between B and C varying according to the levels of A; or as the association between A and C varying according to the levels of B. In general, one would select the causally prior variable to be the one which affects the association between the other two, but often it is not easy to determine which of the three is in fact causally prior.

Now that we have noted all these difficulties and problems, let us see how much headway we can make with a causal analysis. Cowart (1973), in a study of electoral choice, looked at the influences on voting for US Senators in statewide elections. He chose three variables to cross-tabulate with voting, either Democratic or Republican. The first was the voters' basic party identification – essentially, whether they thought of themselves as Democrats, Republicans, or Independents. The second variable indicated whether one or other of the candidates was an incumbent, fighting to retain his position. This variable had three categories: one of the candidates was a Democratic incumbent, one of the candidates was a Republican incumbent, or neither candidate was an incumbent. The third variable he included concerned the voters' attitudes towards the parties' policies on domestic issues and towards the parties as managers of government. The data, obtained from a series of four surveys of US national samples over the period 1956–68, is shown in Table 9.1. Although Cowart makes some causal inferences from this data in his paper, he neither uses loglinear analysis nor attempts a causal model. We shall follow through the development of a causal model applied to his data to illustrate the techniques involved.

Table 9.1   *Voting for US Senators, by Incumbent's Party, Attitude to Party Performance and Party Identification*

Party identification	Attitude	Incumbency	Vote D	Vote R
D	D	D	288	25
D	D	No	139	18
D	D	R	193	37
D	N	D	185	18
D	N	No	83	15
D	N	R	99	31
D	R	D	49	20
D	R	No	29	14
D	R	R	38	29
I	D	D	48	13
I	D	No	14	6
I	D	R	27	21
I	N	D	81	51
I	N	No	20	29
I	N	R	50	70
I	R	D	30	51
I	R	No	18	39
I	R	R	21	63
R	D	D	7	19
R	D	No	2	8
R	D	R	4	28
R	N	D	20	63
R	N	No	13	49
R	N	R	19	88
R	R	D	23	155
R	R	No	13	129
R	R	R	14	227

Key:
D – Democrat; I – Independent; R – Republican; N – neutral; No – no incumbent.
Source: Cowart, 1973, table 2.

The first necessity is to determine some causal ordering between the four variables. Immediately, one can see that there is room for debate about an appropriate causal sequence. Nevertheless, we shall take party identification and incumbency as joint predictor variables, hypothesising some relationship between them, but not committing ourselves to its direction. Party identification is taken as a predictor on the ground that this is a fairly stable feature of people's political values, one which usually would have been established long before voting. We shall assume that these predictors causally influence both partisan attitudes to domestic issues and management ability, and voting. Moreover, we shall assume that partisan attitude is causally prior to voting. This last assumption is in accord with common sense – what one thinks of the parties' policies and competence affects one's vote – but common sense is not an infallible guide. It could be argued, for instance, that these attitudes were measured in interview some time *after* the votes had been cast, and the way one votes might affect how one subsequently judges the competence of parties.

We shall, however, stick with the assumption that attitude influences voting, relying on the argument that although the attitudes were indeed measured after the votes were cast, attitudes are unlikely to have shifted sharply from those held before the elections took place. These considerations lead us to the causal model diagrammed in Figure 9.4, in which all the possible two-variable causal relationships which could exist, given the causal sequence we have settled on, have been indicated. There might also be interactions, but including these too would have made the diagram difficult to follow. The primary task of our loglinear analysis will be to pare down to the minimum the number of causal influences or 'paths' shown in the diagram by eliminating those which are not needed to fit the data. This will involve the examination of a number of separate loglinear models, one after the other.

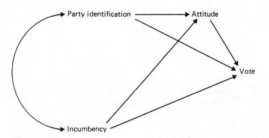

Figure 9.4   *Causal model, showing all possible two-variable paths for US Senatorial elections data.*

Starting at the left-hand edge of the diagram, we can ask whether there is actually a significant association between the two predictor variables – in other words, is the curved arrow really necessary? A moment's thought will show that this question can be answered by examining data relating only to the predictors, party identification and incumbency, and that we can ignore the other two variables for now because we have assumed that they exert no causal influence on the predictors. Hence, they cannot have any influence on the association.

As we noted in Chapter 8, the relationship between two variables ignoring all others is known as the marginal relationship. To examine this relationship, we need to fit a model of no association to the marginal table of party identification by incumbency, Table 9.2. Since the model fails to fit, we conclude that there is an association between the two predictors, the magnitude of which is indicated by the uncertainty coefficient value of 0·007.

Table 9.2 *Relationship between Party Identification (P) and Incumbency (I) from a Marginal Table of the US Senatorial Elections Data*

Party identification Incumbency	Democrat	Independent	Republican
Democrat/Republican challenger	585	274	287
No incumbent	303	126	214
Republican/Democratic challenger	427	252	380

Fitting model $[P][I]$ to table gives:
$G^2 = 41 \cdot 0$ $Df = 4$ Significance: 0%

The next step is to look at the relationship between the two predictors and partisan attitude. Any relationships between these three and voting may be ignored, since we have supposed that voting does not influence them. Therefore, we can fit models to the marginal table for the three variables (Table 9.3). We are no longer interested in the relationship between party identification and incumbency; we now want to focus solely on the relationships between this pair of variables and attitude. If we include the term [Party identification, Incumbency] in our models, it will take care of the association between the predictors, leaving us free to model the other relationships. Fitting each of the four models which includes the effect $[P,I]$ gives the results shown at the bottom of Table 9.3. The simplest model which provides an adequate fit is the second, indicating that there are associations between the party identification and attitude variables, but no significant association between incumbency and attitude, nor any interaction. Thus, so far, we have been able to eliminate one of the causal paths shown in Figure 9.5.

Table 9.3   *Relationship between Party Identification (P), Incumbency (I) and Partisan Attitude (A)*

Partisan attitude	Incumbency	Party identification		
		D	I,	R
D	D	313	61	26
D	N	162	20	10
D	R	230	48	32
N	D	203	132	83
N	N	98	49	62
N	R	130	120	107
R	D	69	81	178
R	N	43	57	142
R	R	67	84	241

Results of fitting models to the above data:

	Model	G^2	Df	Significance (%)
(1)	$[P,I][P,A][I,A]$	10	8	28
(2)	$[P,I][P,A]$	18	12	11
(3)	$[P,I]$ $[I,A]$	846	12	0
(4)	$[P,I]$	874	18	0

Key:
D – Democrat, I – Independent, N – neutral, R – Republican.

The final step in the analysis is to examine the relationships between voting and the other three variables. We use the full table for this, and fit models including the three-way interaction between party identification, incumbency and attitude. This interaction term takes care of all (for the moment) irrelevant relationships amongst these three variables, leaving the relationships between them and voting as the focus of attention. There are four models we can fit which include this interaction, but no other interactions, and these are shown in Table 9.4. The first model fits very well, so other interaction effects are not needed in the model, but this is the only one which does fit. Thus, there are associations between voting and each of the other three variables.

Figure 9.5 shows the results of our efforts. Voting seems to depend on the voter's attitude to the political parties, on whether the incumbent is standing for re-election and on the voter's allegiance to

Table 9.4   *Results of Fitting Models to Detect Relationships between Voting and Other Variables in the US Senatorial Elections Data (Table 9.1)*

	Model				G^2	Df	Significance (%)
(1)	$[P,I,A]$	$[V,I]$	$[V,P]$	$[V,A]$	12	20	92
(2)	$[P,I,A]$		$[V,P]$	$[V,A]$	62	22	0
(3)	$[P,I,A]$	$[V,I]$		$[V,A]$	676	22	0
(4)	$[P,I,A]$	$[V,I]$	$[V,P]$		126	22	0

a party. Furthermore, amongst those who identify with each of the parties, the voter's attitude concerning the competence of the parties on domestic issues and on their ability to manage the work of government depends on the voter's party identification, but not on the party of the incumbent.

Following the procedure outlined in Chapter 8, we can find the strengths of each of the associations, measuring them with the uncertainty coefficient, and place the values on the causal diagram as in Figure 9.5. The figures give an indication of the relative strengths of the causal influences on the variables. One can see that the strongest influence on the choice of whom to vote for is one's party allegiance, and this factor also has a powerful effect on one's attitude to the parties. The other variables have a much weaker effect on voting. It is interesting that the causal relationship between what the voters think of the parties' competence and how they vote is so weak.

Figure 9.5 resembles a 'path diagram' such as might be generated using path analysis (Duncan, 1966), but the similarity is only

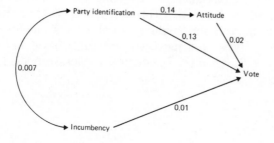

Figure 9.5   *Causal model for US Senatorial elections data; figures are values of the uncertainty coefficient.*

superficial. The difference between the figure and a path diagram lies in the fact that, using path coefficients, the total causal effect of one variable on another can be assessed by summing the products of the coefficients on each of the paths connecting the two variables. This is *not* possible using loglinear techniques and the uncertainty coefficient. Moreover, it is not possible to assign a value equivalent to the 'unexplained variance' which occurs in path analysis. Thus, at the present state of the art, techniques for the analysis of categorical data in terms of causal models are not yet as powerful as those available for the analysis of interval data.

Summary

Loglinear analysis can only be used to discover the strengths of relationships; it cannot be used to determine which variables are causes and which effects. Hence, the first step of a causal analysis is to specify a causal ordering. Successive loglinear models, each in turn including more predictor variables, are then used to examine the strengths of the causal paths. However, the causal analysis of categorical variables cannot (yet) deal easily with interactions and has no technique equivalent to the path coefficient calculus of regression-based path analysis.

Further Reading

Good introductions to the logic of causal analysis are provided in Blalock (1964) and Hirschi and Selvin (1973). Techniques for causal analysis based on the multiple regression of interval level variables (for example, path analysis) are described in Heise (1975), and in Duncan (1975b), the latter also covering their application to non-recursive models. Boudon (1974) and Davis (1971) present other analytical techniques for handling causal models: the former using correlation analysis, and the latter, measures based on Yule's Q. Fienberg (1977, chapter 7), discusses causal modelling using loglinear analysis.

10

Partitioning Tables

This chapter will be concerned with a rather different kind of loglinear model from those we have so far encountered. The new models enable one to divide a data table into a number of partitions, and then fit each partition separately. As we shall see, such models are particularly powerful tools for investigating problems of social mobility, intergenerational change and, indeed, change generally. However, before introducing the partitioning technique, we must review the way one deals with data tables in which one or a few of the cells are known to be 'special', because, for instance, their frequencies are fixed by design.

Structural Values

Data tables sometimes include cells whose frequencies we know before any data is collected. For instance, in a cross-classification of criminals by the crime with which they have been convicted and their sex, we know immediately that the cell corresponding to 'rape by females' will be empty. Likewise, in a table of delinquency by age, the cell corresponding to delinquents under 11 years old will be empty since young children are not legally responsible for their 'criminal' acts. Such prespecifiable cell values are known as *structural* values (or 'structural zeros', since the fixed value is commonly zero). By no means all zero cells in a data table are structural zeros; only those in which a zero frequency is a logical necessity. Cells in which no observations have been entered because the sample happened not to include members with that combination of categories are known as 'sampling zeros'.

Distinguishing structural from sampling values is important, because structural values place constraints on the model table. For instance, a model table to fit the crime/sex data which included a number of 'female rapists' would clearly not be satisfactory. One must, therefore, constrain the model table so that it has the appropriate frequencies in the structural cells. Fortunately, this is fairly easy to achieve using the iterative scaling procedure. One simply arranges for the structural cells to be avoided when performing the scaling. The iterative scaling proceeds as though the structural cells were absent from the table; their values have no influence at all on the calculation of the other frequencies.

The presence of structural cells does, however, affect the degrees of freedom of the model. The degrees of freedom are reduced by one as compared with the 'normal' number for every structural value in the data. This rule works if there is only one structural value in the data table. It also works if there are more, provided that the structural values happen to be arranged in the table in such a way that no marginal table includes more than one frequency obtained by summing over structural values. If this condition is not met, the adjustments to the degrees of freedom that are needed are less straightforward to calculate. Bishop, Fienberg and Holland (1975) discuss these awkward cases in detail.

Detecting Outliers

One useful application of the concept of structural values is in detecting the presence of *outliers*. An outlier is a cell having a frequency which seems to be out of line with the rest of the data, judging by its large residual obtained from an otherwise reasonably closely fitting model. The same model may be fitted again with the cell in question treated as structural. In this way one skirts around the possible outlier, but fits the rest of the data. The difference in G square between the two fits, one with the structural value and one without, is distributed as chi square with one degree of freedom. If the resulting significance level is large, the suspect cell is indeed an outlier.

As an example, consider Table 10.1, showing the frequency of church attendance of a national sample of Catholics by sex (Hornsby-Smith and Lee, 1979). The residuals (section (b) in Table 10.1) make it clear that the proportion of female frequent churchgoers is larger (and the proportion of male frequent attenders, smaller) than would be expected under an assumption that attendance does not depend on sex. Making the 'several times a month/female' cell structural, yields the residual table shown at the bottom of Table 10.1. Note that the structural cell has a residual of zero, and that the degrees of freedom is reduced by one as compared with the initial independence model to allow for the additional constraint imposed on the fitting. The second model fits much better than the first; indeed, it fits the data rather well. Since there are only two categories of sex, exactly the same analysis could be carried out, with similar results, by making the corresponding male cell structural.

The scale of the difference that making the cell structural has caused can be quantified by referring the difference in G square between the two models $(30 \cdot 1 - 2 \cdot 1)$ with one degree of freedom to the chi square distribution. The frequent attender/female cell does seem to be an outlier: there are significantly more female (and less male) frequent churchgoers than would be expected from the frequencies in the rest of the table. To explain this finding, one would have to look closely at the culture and traditions of Catholic

Table 10.1   *Frequency of Roman Catholic Church Attendance by Sex*

(a) *Data*

Attendance	Male	Female
At least several times a month	195	358
Now and again	85	99
Christmas, Easter and special occasions	110	99
Never or practically never	110	99

(b) *Standardised residuals from a simple independence model*
$G^2 = 30 \cdot 1$ $Df = 3$ Significance: 0%

Attendance	Male	Female
At least several times a month	$-2 \cdot 9$	$2 \cdot 5$
Now and again	$0 \cdot 6$	$0 \cdot 5$
Christmas, Easter and special occasions	$2 \cdot 1$	$-1 \cdot 8$
Never or practically never	$2 \cdot 1$	$-1 \cdot 8$

(c) *Standardised residuals from an independence model with one cell defined as structural*
$G^2 = 2 \cdot 1$ $Df = 2$ Significance: 35%

Attendance	Male	Female
At least several times a month	$0 \cdot 0$	$0 \cdot 0$
Now and again	$-0 \cdot 9$	$0 \cdot 9$
Christmas, Easter and special occasions	$0 \cdot 4$	$-0 \cdot 4$
Never or practically never	$0 \cdot 4$	$-0 \cdot 4$

Source: Hornsby-Smith and Lee, 1979, table 3.8.

families. In general, the inferences one draws from finding outliers are either that the particular levels of the variables pertaining to that cell interact in combination in a way not expected from their joint effect on the rest of the table, or that there has been an error in collecting the data for that cell.

Partitioning

An extension of the idea of structural values leads to a technique for analysing a data table with the help of models in which the data is *partitioned* into two or more sections, each of which is fitted separately. We shall describe these new models, using first a section of the data that was introduced in Chapter 7.

Table 10.2 shows one marginal table from the data on perceptions of relative financial circumstances: a cross-tabulation of how respondents felt their present finances compared with those of other US families, by how they thought their parents' families situation compared when they were aged 16. The table is an example of a common kind of data, in which the same concept is measured at two points in time and then cross-tabulated. In this respect it resembles a social mobility table, in which parents' occupation, status, or class is tabulated against respondents' occupation, status, or class.

There is little we can do to explore this table using the techniques we have discussed so far. We can test for the main effects of the variables (both highly significant) and for the association between the variables (also highly significant), but these results are to be

Table 10.2   *Perceptions of Family Income in Comparison with that of Other Families, When Aged 16, by When Interviewed*

| Income when aged 16 | Current income | | | | |
	Far below average	Below average	Average	Above average	Far above average
Far below average	105	133	155	39	9
Below average	237	815	1,065	185	26
Average	339	1,225	3,536	571	63
Above average	73	353	861	478	34
Far above average	6	26	53	38	21

Source: ICPSR, 1972–8.

expected from the nature of the variables and are not especially interesting on their own. All they tell us is that respondents' answers about their current financial position are not independent of their responses about their parents' financial position.

Nevertheless, the standardised residuals shown in Table 10.3 obtained from fitting an independence model are interesting, revealing a marked pattern. There are large positive residuals in the cells lying along the leading diagonal of the table, the cells in which respondents who said their family circumstances had not changed would be placed. Perhaps there is something special about those who feel they are still in the same circumstances as when they were young.

Table 10.3   *Standardised Residuals from Fitting a Model of Simple Independence to the Data of Table 10.2*

No association model, no partitions:
$G^2 = 847$ $Df = 16$ Significance: 0%

Income when aged 16	Far below average	Below average	Current income Average	Above average	Far above average
Far below average	12·9	2·4	− 5·5	− 2·2	1·0
Below average	5·2	10·3	− 5·6	− 6·3	− 1·4
Average	− 3·8	− 4·7	7·6	− 5·5	− 2·3
Above average	− 5·1	− 4·1	− 3·7	16·8	1·5
Far above average	− 1·4	− 1·6	− 2·9	4·7	13·0

This possibility can be investigated with a second 'independence' model, which differs from the first in that the leading diagonal cells are defined to be structural. This device causes the diagonal cells to be omitted from the fitting, so allowing the level of association in the off-diagonal cells to be examined alone. In effect, the table is broken into two partitions, one containing the diagonal cells, and the other all the off-diagonal cells. The first partition consists of the cells including those who say their financial circumstances have remained the same, and the second partition those who say their circumstances have changed.

Table 10.4   *Standardised Residuals from Fitting a Model of Quasi-Independence*

No association model, leading diagonal as one partition, rest of table as another
$G^2 = 139$ $Df = 11$ Significance: 0%

Income when aged 16	Far below average	Below average	Current income Average	Above average	Far above average
Far below average	0·0	3·9	− 2·7	− 0·5	1·4
Below average	6·0	0·0	− 0·6	− 3·4	− 1·0
Average	− 1·5	0·2	0·0	1·3	− 1·1
Above average	− 4·1	− 1·8	2·5	0·0	2·3
Far above average	− 1·2	− 1·2	− 1.6	6·2	0·0

The result of fitting this model (known as a 'quasi-independence' model) is disappointing (Table 10.4) – it does not fit any better than the simple independence model. Incidentally, one can see that the degrees of freedom of this model are less than that of the first independence model, in order to account for the additional constraints on the fit resulting from the introduction of the five structural cells. Note also that, because we have defined the diagonal cells to be structural, the model frequencies in these cells are set to those in the data table and, hence, the residuals along the diagonal are all zero.

Despite the lack of improvement of fit, we shall persist, trying next a slightly more complicated partitioned model. This is one in which those who say their financial position has improved, and those who say that it has got worse, are each treated separately. The table must be broken up into three partitions, as indicated in Table 10.5, and each partition fitted in turn. Partition 0 is composed of structural cells, so the fitted table frequencies for these cells must be equal to the corresponding data cell frequencies. The partition 1 cells are fitted by *temporarily* defining all the rest of the table to be structural, so that only the cells in this partition are fitted by the iterative scaling procedure. Partition 2 is fitted similarly by declaring all the cells in partitions 0 and 1 to be structural. The overall G square and degrees of freedom of the model as a whole are calculated by adding together those obtained from fitting each

Table 10.5   *Partitioning Design for Model 3*

		Current income			
Income when aged 16	*Far below average*	*Below average*	*Average*	*Above average*	*Far above average*
Far below average	0	1	1	1	1
Below average	2	0	1	1	1
Average	2	2	0	1	1
Above average	2	2	2	0	1
Far above average	2	2	2	2	0

Table 10.6   *The Fit of the Partitions Making up Model 3*

	G^2	Df	
Partition 0	0·0	0	(fits perfectly)
Partition 1	9·3	3	
Partition 2	5·1	3	
Overall	14·5	6	Significance: 2·4%

partition (see Table 10.6). This third model fits the data more closely, but the residuals again show an interesting pattern (Table 10.7). The larger residuals tend to occur in the bottom left- and top right-hand corners of the table, in the cells in which those respondents who have experienced great changes in their financial position would be placed. This suggests that a fourth model might fit even better.

Table 10.7   *Standardised Residuals from Fitting Model 3*

No association model, partitioned as in Table 10.5
$G^2 = 14·5$ $Df = 6$ Significance: 2·4%

		Current income			
Income when aged 16	*Far below average*	*Below average*	*Average*	*Above average*	*Far above average*
Far below average	0·0	0·0	− 1·0	1·3	2·6
Below average	0·0	0·0	0·4	− 1·0	0·3
Average	0·9	− 0·4	0·0	0·3	− 0·8
Above average	− 1·7	0·7	0·1	0·0	0·0
Far above average	0·0	0·7	− 0·5	0·0	0·0

This treats separately (see Table 10.8):

Partition 0 – those whose financial position is felt to be unchanged
from when they were aged 16;
Partition 1 – those who have moved up or down one category;
Partition 2 – those who have moved down more than one category;
Partition 3 – those who have moved up more than one category.

Table 10.8   *Partitioning Design for Model 4*

Income when aged 16	Current income				
	Far below average	Below average	Average	Above average	Far above average
Far below average	0	1	2	2	2
Below average	1	0	1	2	2
Average	3	1	0	1	2
Above average	3	3	1	0	1
Far above average	3	3	3	1	0

The fit is, indeed, much better, as shown in Table 10.9. The residuals remaining when this model is fitted are all very much less than one, except for the one in the top right-hand cell. In any case, we are now at the end of the road, for the last model had only one degree of freedom. More complex partitioned models which impose

Table 10.9   *Standardised Residuals from Fitting Model 4*

No association model, partitioned as in Table 10.8
$G^2 = 1 \cdot 3$ $Df = 1$ Significance: $24 \cdot 5 \%$

Income when aged 16	Current income				
	Far below average	Below average	Average	Above average	Far above average
Far below average	0·0	0·0	0·0	− 0·4	1·0
Below average	0·0	0·0	0·0	0·2	− 0·5
Average	0·0	0·0	0·0	0·0	0·0
Above average	0·0	0·0	0·0	0·0	0·0
Far above average	0·2	0·1	0·0	0·0	0·0

further constraints on the fit would have zero degrees of freedom and would, therefore, necessarily fit exactly. Since their perfect fit can be predicted beforehand, they would tell us nothing new about the data.

The results we have obtained can be interpreted as follows. The fitted table derived from model 1, the model with no association and no partitions, shows the cell frequencies which would be expected if a respondent's present financial situation were entirely independent of his reported past situation at age 16. But model 1 failed to fit the data, meaning that the present situation does depend on the past. In particular, the residual table (Table 10.5) shows that the probability that an individual's current situation is the same as in the past is disproportionately large compared with what would be predicted from the independence model.

We next tried model 2, a model which attempted to fit only the off-diagonal cells of the data table. Here we are testing the idea that, aside from those individuals who have experienced no change, one's present financial situation is independent of one's past situation. This model did not fit either, and our third attempt therefore dealt separately with those who felt better off as compared with when they were 16, and those who felt worse off. Within each of these two groups, we hypothesised that the present situation in which the respondents found themselves was not dependent on their past situation. In other words, we proposed that once an individual has decided that he is better or worse off than in the past, the extent of the perceived change is independent of the particular past situation. This model fitted more closely than the previous ones, but still not well.

Model 4 differed from model 3 only in that those who felt a change of one step along the scale of financial standing were treated as a separate group. In this group the respondent's current position is independent of his past, in the sense that there is an equal probability of him moving either up or down one category. This last model fitted the data very well.

The technique of fitting partitioned models has been applied with interesting results to intergenerational social mobility tables, in which the variables are father's and son's status (Blau and Duncan, 1967). The simple independence model does not fit most social mobility tables because, as with the data just examined, it leaves large residuals along the leading diagonal. This is a sign of what Goodman (1965a) calls 'status persistence' or 'status inheritance',

Table 10.10   *Switching of Religious Affiliation: Religion of Destination by Religion of Origin, Heads of Households from NORC Data, 1975–6*

Religion at age 16	High SES	Medium SES	Bap- tist	Low SES	Current religion Protes- tant, no denom- ination	Cath- olic	Jew	Other	None
High SES	157	24	3	7	15	7	0	3	23
Medium SES	37	466	45	39	28	21	2	5	51
Baptist	20	44	468	19	19	12	0	2	38
Low SES	10	18	13	83	11	6	0	0	9
Protestant, no denomination	5	4	2	2	32	2	0	1	8
Catholic	12	26	10	10	5	622	1	2	70
Jewish	1	1	0	1	0	1	45	0	6
Other	0	0	0	0	0	3	0	15	2
None	6	19	9	6	4	5	0	1	45

Source: derived from Newport, 1979, table 2.

the tendency for sons to remain in the same status category as their fathers.

Another interesting example, also based on data from NORC (ICPSR, 1975, 1976) is reported in Newport (1979). The focus of Newport's study was on 'religious switchers': those who had changed their religious faith from the one in which they were originally brought up. A mobility matrix, that is, a cross-tabulation of religious affiliation when aged 16 by affiliation at the time of interview, was analysed using the quasi-independence model mentioned above. Newport's data is reproduced in Table 10.10. The Protestant denominational categories in this table were chosen by combining denominations according to the similarity of their adherents' socioeconomic status (SES), a technique which Newport argues gives reasonably homogeneous categories, and which is necessary because there are many hundreds of different denominations, each represented by only a few respondents in the sample.

Table 10.11 shows the residuals obtained by fitting a quasi-independence model to this data. (Newport uses mobility ratios, the ratios of the expected to observed frequencies, rather than standardised residuals, but both lead to the same substantive conclusions.) From the residuals, we can see that there is more movement from the Catholic faith to no faith than would be expected from the model. That is, more people are giving up their Catholic faith and not adopting another than would be expected if 'switchers' adopted a new faith independently of the one they were leaving. Furthermore, high-status Protestants tend not to switch to low-status denominations or to the Baptists; instead they tend to leave particular denominations, whilst remaining Protestant more often than expected. Medium- and low-status Protestant denomination members tend to abandon their religion in favour of no religion less often than expected.

Table 10.11 *Standardised Residuals from Fitting a Model of Quasi-Independence to the Data of Table 10.10*

Religion at age 16	High SES	Medium SES	Baptist	Low SES	Protestant, no denomination	Catholic	Jew	Other	None
High SES	0·0	0·6	− 2·3	− 0·8	2·1	0·0	− 0·6	1·3	0·0
Medium SES	0·6	0·0	1·9	1·6	0·0	− 0·3	1·0	0·2	− 2·7
Baptist	0·0	0·7	0·0	0·3	0·6	− 0·4	− 0·8	− 0·4	− 0·8
Low SES	0·5	0·2	1·5	0·0	1·5	0·1	− 0·5	− 1·1	− 2·3
Protestant, no denomination	1·1	− 0·8	− 0·6	− 0·4	0·0	0·0	− 0·3	0·9	0·5
Catholic	− 1·2	− 1·3	− 1·7	− 1·3	− 2·4	0·0	0·7	− 0·2	5·4
Jewish	− 0·1	− 0·9	− 1·1	0·0	− 1·0	0·3	0·0	− 0·4	2·2
Other	− 0·8	− 1·1	− 0·8	− 0·7	− 0·7	4·2	− 0·1	0·0	0·6
None	− 0·6	1·1	0·5	− 0·3	− 0·9	0·0	0·5	0·0	0·0

Although the examples we have used are variations on the theme of social mobility, there is no reason for the partitioning technique to be confined to this kind of data. It can be applied to tables which are not 'square' and to tables including more than two variables. Indeed, partitioning may be appropriate and useful whenever there is reason to believe that certain combinations of categories of variables have consequences different in kind to those of other combinations.

Summary

Tables with 'special' cells may be analysed by preserving those cells from modification by the iterative proportional scaling algorithm.

This technique can be used with advantage in dealing with structural cells, that is, cells in which the frequency is fixed by design, for detecting outliers (cells with unusually low or high frequencies) and as the basis for partitioned models. Partitioning involves the fitting of a model to a number of sections of the data table in turn, each fit being independent of the others. Partitioned models are particularly powerful for the analysis of mobility, but may be useful in other contexts also.

Further Reading

Hauser (1980) provides an introduction to the use of partitioned models to investigate social mobility. Bishop, Fienberg and Holland (1975, chapter 5) give many examples of partitioned (or 'incomplete') tables. Duncan (1975a) shows how partitioning may be used to study the effect of the individual cells of a table.

11

The Mathematical Basis

Now that we have a good idea of the way to use loglinear analysis, it is time to consider why the procedures work. The presentation so far has intentionally not been in terms of the mathematical foundations of the technique because, for the practitioner, this initially gets in the way of understanding how to use it. Nevertheless, both because it is unwise to use a technique without any idea of why it works, and because appreciation of some features of loglinear analysis require a more detailed understanding of its basis, this chapter presents a brief overview of the derivation of the loglinear model. Be warned, however, that if you have no mathematical background at all, you may find this chapter hard going in parts. A much more comprehensive and rigorous account of the theory of loglinear analysis can be found in Bishop, Fienberg and Holland (1975). In the first part of the chapter, we shall develop an equation for a loglinear model to fit a simple '2 by 2' table. Later we shall be able to extend this to cover tables including more cells and more variables.

As was shown in earlier chapters, a two-dimensional table may include one or more of four effects: the grand mean, the main effect of one variable (say, variable A), the main effect of the other variable (variable B), and the association between the two. In its mathematical form, the loglinear model for a two-dimensional table consists of an expression of four terms, known colloquially as u-terms, each representing one of these effects.

We will illustrate the derivation of this loglinear equation with the data shown in Table 11.1 from part of a study of the International Typographical Union. This cross-tabulates the number of printers who worked on day or night shift with whether they ever visited the homes of the printers with whom they had become friendly. Lipset *et al.* (1956), from whom this table is taken, suggest that although night-shift printers generally associated more with other printers, the disruption of normal family schedules resulting from night work led to fewer making home visits than was the case amongst day-shift printers.

Table 11.1   *Effect of Night-Working by Printers on Visiting Other Printers at Home*

	Night workers	*Day workers*
Do you ever visit other printers at home?		
Yes	141	178
No	58	56

Source: Lipset, Trow and Coleman, 1956, table 13.

The grand mean of the table, for inclusion in the loglinear equation, is calculated by first multiplying together the frequencies in all the cells, then taking a root of the result. For instance, for a '2 by 2' table, one finds the product of the four cell frequencies and then takes the fourth root:

$$\sqrt[4]{x_{11}x_{12}x_{21}x_{22}}$$

$$= (x_{11}x_{12}x_{21}x_{22})^{\frac{1}{4}}$$

Note that taking the fourth root is equivalent to taking the quarterth power. The grand mean is thus based on a geometric, rather than an arithmetic mean. The above expression is rather inconvenient, since it involves products and roots. The logarithm of the expression is, therefore, taken (because this converts products to sums). By convention, natural logarithms are always used. This gives us the expression for the grand mean u-term:

$$u = \tfrac{1}{4}(\log x_{11} + \log x_{12} + \log x_{21} + \log x_{22})$$

This comes to 4·55 for the data of Table 11.1.

Let us leave the u-terms for the main effects for a moment, and deal next with the u-term for association. The magnitude of an association can be measured with the cross-product ratio:

$$cpr = (x_{11}x_{22})/(x_{12}x_{21})$$

and taking logs and the fourth root of this, gives a u-term representing the association:

$$u^{AB}_{11} = \tfrac{1}{4}(\log[x_{11}x_{22}/x_{12}x_{21}])$$

$$= \tfrac{1}{4}(\log x_{11} - \log x_{12} - \log x_{21} + \log x_{22})$$

which, for the data of Table 11.1, equals -0.067.

In fact this is just one of four related association u-terms. The cross-product ratio might have been computed by starting at the bottom right (x_{22}) instead of the top left (x_{11}) corner, giving the same result, but a formula with the subscripts interchanged:

$$cpr = (x_{22}x_{11})/(x_{21}x_{12})$$

Starting from either of the other two cells gives the reciprocal of the cross-product ratio. Corresponding to these four ways of finding the cross-product ratio are four association u-terms, known generically as u^{AB}_{ij}, where for a '2 by 2' table both i and j can take the values 1 or 2. In terms of the example the four related association terms are:

$$u^{AB}_{11} = \tfrac{1}{4}(\quad \log 141 - \log 178 - \log 58 + \log 56) = -0.67$$

$$u^{AB}_{12} = \tfrac{1}{4}(-\log 141 + \log 178 + \log 58 - \log 56) = +0.67$$

$$u^{AB}_{21} = \tfrac{1}{4}(-\log 141 + \log 178 + \log 58 - \log 56) = +0.67$$

$$u^{AB}_{22} = \tfrac{1}{4}(\quad \log 141 - \log 178 - \log 58 + \log 56) = -0.67$$

Now we can deal with the main effect terms. The main effect of a two-level variable is the geometric mean of the frequencies in one category relative to the frequencies in the other category. Thus, the main effect u-term for category 1 of the variable A is given by:

$$u^{A}_{1} = \log[(x_{11}x_{12}/x_{21}x_{22})^{\tfrac{1}{4}}]$$

$$= \tfrac{1}{4}(\log x_{11} + \log x_{12} - \log x_{21} - \log x_{22})$$

The main effect for category 2 of this variable is the same, but 'upside down' – the mean of the frequencies in category 2 relative to those in category 1:

$$u^A_2 = \log\left[(x_{21}x_{22}/x_{11}x_{12})^{\frac{1}{4}}\right]$$

$$= \tfrac{1}{4}(\log x_{11} - \log x_{12} - \log x_{21} + \log x_{22})$$

So

$$u^A_2 = -u^A_1$$

For the 'visiting' variable of Table 11.1, u^A_1 is equal to 0.511. This is the u-term value for the main effect of those visiting printers at home; for those not visiting (u^A_2) the value is -0.511.

The main effect u-term for variable B can be expressed similarly, by finding the mean log relative frequencies of its first and second categories. The u-term for the main effect of night-shift working is -0.495, and for day-shift working is 0.495. Now we can put these u-terms together to form a loglinear equation:

$$\log m_{ij} = u + u^A_i + u^B_j + u^{AB}_{ij}$$

The model frequency (m_{ij}) enters the equation in the log form, because we have taken logs to express the u-terms on the right-hand side. What the equation means is that if we calculate the values of the u-terms for a particular table, using the formulae given above, we can sum them to yield the log of the frequencies which should go in the model table. It is true that we already have a quite adequate method of calculating model table frequencies – iterative proportional scaling – but the equation expresses the loglinear model in the way which shows the basis of the technique most clearly. It also, incidentally, reveals why loglinear analysis is so called: the equation yields a *log* frequency and is *linear* (that is, it contains sums of simple terms).

This equation is rarely used for calculating frequencies. Nevertheless, let us check our computations of the u-term values by obtaining the model cell frequency for the top left-hand corner cell (m_{11}):

$$\log m_{11} = u + u^A_1 + u^B_1 + u^{AB}_{11}$$

$$= 4 \cdot 554 + 0 \cdot 511 - 0 \cdot 050 - 0 \cdot 067$$

$$= 4 \cdot 948$$

$$m_{11} = 140 \cdot 9$$

The equation has regenerated (almost) the original data frequency. The result is not exactly equal to the data cell frequency only because of rounding errors in the calculations. Similarly, the bottom right model cell frequency is given by:

$$\log m_{22} = u + u^A_2 + u^B_2 + u^{AB}_{22}$$

$$= 4 \cdot 554 - 0 \cdot 511 + 0 \cdot 050 - 0 \cdot 067$$

$$= 4 \cdot 025$$

$$m_{22} = 56 \cdot 0$$

Application of the equation has yielded model frequencies almost exactly equal to the data cell frequencies, because we are using the saturated model – that is, the model with all possible terms included. As we noted in a previous chapter, using a 'complete' model always produces a model table identical to the data table, and this is what we are doing here. To generate a model table showing no association, we need only apply the equation omitting the association u-term:

$$\log m_{ij} = u + u^A_i + u^B_j$$

Using this equation, would lead to the same model table as we would obtain fitting the model: [A] [B], using iterative proportional scaling.

Indeed, there is a formal one-to-one correspondence between the terms in a loglinear model equation and the set of effects we would list in a specification of a model for scaling. It is this correspondence which allowed us to describe a model using a set of marginals without needing to know either the underlying equation, or the values of the u-terms. We have discussed the equation for a data table of two dimensions. With higher-dimensional tables, further u-

terms corresponding to interactions and higher-order effects become involved. For example, the interaction u-term in a three-dimensional, eight-celled table is:

$$u^{ABC}_{ijk} = \tfrac{1}{8}(\log [x_{111}x_{221}x_{122}x_{212}/x_{121}x_{211}x_{112}x_{222}])$$

Equations for any particular model can be written down by including one term for each effect in the model. However, not all such equations can be solved using analytic (that is, algebraic) methods. For instance, the equation for a pairwise association model cannot be solved analytically. For such equations the only method of solution is an iterative one, such as iterative proportional scaling.

Some analysts have described data tables by calculating the values of the u-terms in the best-fitting model, and using these values as an indication of the strength of each of the effects. However, u-terms have considerable disadvantages as measures of strength. First, as we saw when calculating u-terms for the '2 by 2' table about printers, a u-term will often actually consist of several coefficients. The main effect term for printers working night shift (u^B_1) was -0.494, and for day-shift workers (u^B_2), 0.494. There will always be a coefficient for each degree of freedom of the marginal table corresponding to the effect to which the u-term relates, so we often have to deal not with simple, single values, but with matrices of coefficients. Secondly, the u-terms are based on a log scale (they are calculated from log frequencies) and are, therefore, rather difficult to interpret in a sociologically meaningful way.

Multiplicative and Additive Models

It was shown above that the basic loglinear equation consists of a sum of u-terms equated to log model frequencies. We could take antilogs to convert back from the log to the original scale to yield an equation consisting of a product of antilogs of the u-terms equated to the straight model frequencies. Since the u-terms themselves are composed of data cell frequencies multiplied and divided, it should be clear why the loglinear model is described as 'multiplicative'. Moreover, the effects described and tested using the loglinear method are themselves products of ratios of frequencies. For instance, association in loglinear analysis is defined by the cross-product ratio.

However, other models have often been used by social

researchers that are based on additive rather than multiplicative functions of cell frequencies. Such models define effects in terms of sums and differences of proportions rather than products of ratios. For instance, Table 11.2 shows the data of Table 11.1 percentaged down columns. Because the two columns will hold identical percentages if there is no association, we could use the difference between the percentages across the table instead of the cross-product ratio as a measure of association. Thus, in this table one could take 76 per cent minus 71 per cent, equals 5 per cent, as an indicator of the amount of association. Indeed, this is often done to assess the association in a percentaged table quickly and roughly. Coleman (1970) has built up a system of analysis based on percentage differences which has much the same goals as loglinear analysis.

Table 11.2   *Data of Table 11.1, Percentaged*

	Night workers (%)	Day workers (%)
Do you ever visit other printers at home?		
Yes	71	76
No	29	24
	(191)	(234)

One difficulty with having these two alternative methods of analysis is that they can give different, and sometimes contradictory results. A singularly clear example of this occurs with some data published by Brown and Harris (1978), shown in Table 11.3. Brown was interested in the social origins of depression and suggested that depression amongst women was due to the interaction of the presence of a 'vulnerability factor' and the occurrence of a 'provoking agent'. For example, according to Brown's thesis, a woman is likely to be depressed if she lacks intimacy with a husband or boyfriend (the vulnerability factor) *and* is experiencing marital difficulties (the provoking agent). Neither lack of intimacy, nor marital difficulties, on their own are likely to cause depression.

To test this thesis, we must look for an interaction between the presence or absence of depression (a variable Brown calls 'caseness'), the existence of a vulnerability factor and the existence of a provoking agent. Table 11.3 shows an example of these variables cross-tabulated for the 'lack of intimacy' vulnerability

Table 11.3   *Number of Women in Camberwell Developing Depression (Caseness) in a One-Year Period by the Presence of a Provoking Agent and a Vulnerability Factor, Lack of Intimacy*

	Lack of intimacy with husband or boyfriend			
	Yes		No	
Severe event	Yes	No	Yes	No
Case	24	2	9	2
Not case	52	60	79	191

Source: Brown and Harris, 1978.

factor. Since we are interested in interaction, we want to know whether the association in the left-hand partial table is the same as that in the right-hand one. If the associations are significantly different, the data corroborates Brown's theory.

The cross-product ratios for the two partial tables (13·8 for the left-hand, and 10·8 for the right-hand table) are similar in magnitude, indicating the absence of much interaction. Therefore, as one would expect, a pairwise association loglinear model fits the data very well. On the other hand, if the table is percentaged down (by 'caseness'), the differences in percentage of those exhibiting 'caseness' between those experiencing a severe event and those not doing so for the left-hand partial table is 29 per cent, and for the right-hand table is 9 per cent. Since 29 per cent is so much larger than 9 per cent, it is natural to conclude, as Brown did, that there is interaction (Everitt and Smith, 1979).

Thus, the two methods for assessing interaction give different results. This is because the methods are based on different definitions of association and interaction: one multiplicative, and one additive. It is not possible to rule that one definition is necessarily superior to the other. With the multiplicative model, we are looking at the number of those depressed relative to the number not depressed; with the additive model, the focus is on the number of those depressed as a proportion of the whole sample. It is very difficult to decide which of these is more appropriate, for good arguments in favour of both can be made (Darroch, 1974). Pragmatically, one might opt for a multiplicative model on the ground that more powerful and convenient methods, such as loglinear analysis, are available for multiplicative models, work on additive models being still relatively undeveloped (Grizzle, Starmer and Koch, 1969).

Summary

An equation can be constructed to express model table frequencies in terms of a linear function of log frequencies. Such loglinear equations are the foundation of loglinear analysis. The equations are built from u-terms, each of which is a matrix of coefficients formed from various products and ratios of log frequencies. Association and interaction can be seen from these equations to be defined in a multiplicative form; alternative, additive definitions are also possible, but analytic methods based on these are not well developed.

Further Reading

Fienberg (1977), Reynolds (1977a) and Bishop, Fienberg and Holland (1975), all further develop the mathematics introduced in this chapter. Reynolds is probably the easiest to begin with. Comparisons of loglinear analysis with other techniques for qualitative data are to be found in Goodman (1975), Knokke (1975), Gillespie (1977) and Swafford (1980).

12

Computer Programs

The techniques we have discussed in this book are all but impossible to perform entirely by hand. The effort required is so great that the only practicable means of carrying out analyses on data sets of realistic size is by computer. Fortunately there are a number of proven computer programs which can be used to carry out the necessary arithmetical labour.

Computers have already become nearly universal in quantitative social research, because they are so effective at managing large amounts of data. Even a fairly modest survey of 200 respondents asked fifty questions will generate 10,000 items of information, Keeping track of these requires enormous effort, unless one is assisted by a computer. Moreover, computers are much less prone to error than humans when dealing with routine tasks. A 'package' such as SPSS (Statistical Package for the Social Sciences) enables one to store data in an identifiable and convenient form, as well as to generate frequency distributions and cross-tabulations with very little trouble.

Once one has access to a computer for data management, it is but a small step to using it for analysis as well. Indeed, SPSS can be used directly for the more common analytic procedures, because it includes routines to perform multiple regression, analysis of variance and other techniques in the 'general linear modelling' family (Nie *et al.*, 1975). At present, however, it does not include facilities for loglinear analysis. Nevertheless, SPSS will generate cross-tabulations from raw data, which can then be entered into a loglinear analysis program. Described below are three of the more popular programs for performing loglinear analysis. They vary mainly in the way in which the user enters his data and in the algorithm they use to fit models. But there is not a great deal to choose between them, unless one needs a special facility which not all provide. If the locally available computer already has a suitable program, you are probably best advised to use that rather than attempt to obtain a perhaps marginally more suitable or convenient alternative.

All three programs are written in FORTRAN and, therefore, should be suitable for almost any make or model of computer. The only restriction is that two of the programs (ECTA and GLIM) are very large (in part because they are capable of handling very large tables, and in part also because they are very sophisticated); and some small computers may not have adequate memory capacity. The transfer of a program from one computer to another is rarely completely straightforward and is best left to a professional programmer.

Data analysis programs are used either in batch, or interactive mode. In batch mode, the data is prepared in advance, often on punched cards, and then submitted to the computer. After running the program, the results are returned to the user minutes or hours later. In the interactive mode, the user enters commands to the program via a terminal and the program reacts immediately, or nearly so. Because one is interacting directly with the program, it is rather easier to develop and refine a good model using an interactive system than a batch one. On the other hand, an interactive system requires more computer resources and the necessary facilities may not be available at all installations.

At the heart of all these programs is an iterative scaling procedure. A skeletal algorithm to perform loglinear fits by proportional scaling which could be used to write one's own program, has been published by Haberman (1972).

ECTA (Everyman's Contingency Table Analyser)

The program runs in batch mode (although interactive versions have been developed on some computers). It uses the iterative proportional scaling algorithm described in Chapter 5 and will provide the values of the u-terms described in Chapter 11. It is not well suited to fitting partitioned models. Some documentation on using the program is available, but it is rather brief. The program is available from:

Leo A. Goodman, Professor of Statistics and Sociology,
University of Chicago,
1126 East 59th Street,
Illinois 60637, USA

GLIM (Generalised Linear Modelling)

GLIM is a complicated, but very powerful interactive program which can be used for a wide range of analyses in addition to loglinear modelling. It is also possible to run it in batch mode. GLIM will fit models based on linear regression ('ordinary' multiple regression), and logit, probit and loglinear models (Nelder and Wedderburn, 1972). It uses an iterative least-squares algorithm for fitting. Because GLIM is very sophisticated, it requires a reasonably large computer to run it. GLIM is well documented in a lengthy manual. The program is available from:

Numerical Algorithms Group Ltd,
13 Banbury Road,
Oxford, OX2 6NN,
England

LOGLIN

Designed for smaller computer systems, this program is used in the interactive mode. It is similar to ECTA, in that it uses the iterative proportional scaling algorithm, but unlike ECTA, it does have easy to use facilities for fitting partitioned models. On the other hand, it does not calculate u-terms. The screening procedure of Brown (1976) is implemented, and it will calculate the uncertainty coefficients of effects. The program includes a 'Help' command which gives extensive guidance on its use. Little other documentation is available. The program is available from the author:

G. N. Gilbert,
Department of Sociology,
University of Surrey,
Guildford, GU2 5XH,
England

Bibliography

Abell, P., *Model Building in Sociology* (London: Weidenfeld & Nicolson, 1971).

Arber, S. L., and Sawyer, L., 'Changes in the structure of general practice: the patient's viewpoint' (unpublished report to the Department of Health and Social Security, 1979).

Atkins, L., and Jarrett, D., 'The significance of "significance tests" ', in J. Irvine, A. Miles and J. Evans, *Demystifying Social Statistics* (London: Pluto, 1979), pp. 87–110.

Babbie, E. R., *Survey Research Methods* (Belmont, Cal.: Wadsworth, 1973). Chapter 15 is a brief introduction to the elaboration model for examining tables.

Benedetti, J. K., and Brown, M. B., 'Strategies for the selection of log-linear models', *Biometrics*, vol. 34 (1978), pp. 680–6.

Bishop, Y. M. M., Fienberg, S. E., and Holland, P. W., *Discrete Multivariate Analysis* (Cambridge, Mass.: MIT Press, 1975). The most comprehensive reference text on loglinear analysis, dealing with almost all applications of the technique. Uses examples from a number of the biological and social sciences.

Blalock, H. M., *Causal Inferences in Nonexperimental Research* (Chapel Hill, NJ: University of North Carolina, 1964).

Blalock, H. M., 'The measurement problem: a gap between the languages of theory and research', in H. M. Blalock and A. B. Blalock (eds), *Methodology in Social Research* (New York: McGraw-Hill, 1971).

Blalock, H. M., *Social Statistics* (New York: McGraw-Hill, 1979).

Blau, P. M., and Duncan, O. D., *The American Occupational Structure* (New York: Wiley, 1967).

Boudon, R., *The Logic of Sociological Explanation* (Harmondsworth: Penguin, 1974).

Brown, G. W. and Harris, T., *The Social Origins of Depression* (London: Tavistock, 1978).

Brown, M. B., 'Screening effects in multidimensional contingency tables', *Applied Statistics*, vol. 25 (1976), pp. 37–45. Brown introduces the method of screening to locate a good loglinear model.

Cartwright, A., *How Many Children?* (London: Routledge & Kegan Paul, 1976).

Caulcott, E., *Significance Tests* (London: Routledge & Kegan Paul, 1973).

Central Statistical Office, *Social Trends* (London: HMSO, 1976).

Cohen, L. E., and Kleugel, J. R., 'Determinants of juvenile court dispositions: ascriptive and achieved factors in two metropolitan courts', *American Sociological Review*, vol. 43 (1978), pp. 162–76.

Coleman, J., *Introduction to Mathematical Sociology* (Glencoe, Ill.: Free Press, 1964).

Coleman, J., 'Multivariate analysis for attribute data', in E. F. Borgatta and G. W. Bohrnstedt (eds), *Sociological Methodology, 1970* (San Francisco: Jossey-Bass, 1970), pp. 217–45.

Cowart, A. T., 'Electoral choice in American states: incumbency effects, partisan forces and divergent partisan majorities', *American Political Sciences Review*, vol. 67 (1973), pp. 835–53.

Crosby, C., *Intra-Urban Migration*, Papers in Community Studies, No. 17, University of York, 1978.

Darroch, J. W., 'Multiplicative and additive interaction in contingency tables', *Biometrika*, vol. 61 (1974), pp. 207–14.

Davis, J. A., *Elementary Survey Analysis* (Englewood Cliffs, NJ: Prentice-Hall, 1971). Rapidly becomes more than elementary as Davis develops causal models, using a complex set of coefficients based on Yule's Q, but the early chapters include a thorough presentation of the fundamentals of causal modelling.

Davis, J. A., 'Hierarchical models for significance tests in multivariate contingency tables', in H. L. Costner (ed.), *Sociological Methodology* (San Francisco: Jossey-Bass, 1973–4), pp. 189–231. A short introduction to fitting hierarchical loglinear models, particularly focusing on Goodman's approach.

Davis, J. A., 'The loglinear analysis of survey replications', in K. C. Land and S. Spilerman (eds), *Social Indicator Models* (New York: Russell Sage Foundation, 1975), pp. 75–104. Illustrates the use of loglinear analysis on replicated data, obtained by asking the same questions in two or more surveys carried out at different points in time. Davis uses a development of Yule's Q to measure the strengths of effects.

Duncan, O. D., 'Path analysis: sociological examples', *American Journal of Sociology*, vol. 72 (1966), pp. 1–16.

Duncan, O. D., 'Partitioning polytomous variables in multiway contingency analysis', *Social Science Research*, vol. 4 (1975a), pp. 167–82. An interesting development of loglinear analysis to inspect the significance of individual categories of variables in a data table.

Duncan, O. D., *Introduction to Structural Equation Models* (New York: Academic Press, 1975b).

Duncan, O. D., Haller, A. O., and Portes, A., 'Peer influence on aspirations: a reinterpretation', *American Journal of Sociology*, vol. 74 (1968), pp. 119–37.

Erickson, B. H., and Nosanchuk, T. A., *Understanding Data* (Milton Keynes: Open University, 1977). An introduction to 'exploratory data analysis' and Tukey's (1977) techniques written for social researchers.

Everitt, B., *The Analysis of Contingency Tables* (London: Chapman & Hall, 1977). A thorough discussion of contingency tables, including a chapter on loglinear analysis. The examples emphasise medical applications.

Everitt, B., and Smith, A. R. M., 'Interactions in contingency tables: a brief discussion of alternative definitions', *Psychological Medicine*, vol. 9 (1979), pp. 581–3.

Fienberg, S. E., *The Analysis of Cross-Classified Categorical Data* (Cambridge, Mass.: MIT Press, 1977). A clear, if sometimes rather mathematical, introduction to loglinear analysis.

Gillespie, M. W., 'Loglinear techniques and the regression analysis of dummy dependent variables', *Sociological Methods and Research*, vol. 6 (1977), pp. 103–122.

Goldberger, A. S., and Duncan, O. D. (eds), *Structural Equation Models in the Social Sciences* (New York: Seminar Press, 1973).

Goodman, L. A., 'Simultaneous limits for cross-product ratios in contingency tables', *Journal of Royal Statistical Society*, series B, vol. 26 (1964a), pp. 86–102.

Goodman, L. A., 'Simple methods for analyzing three-factor interaction in contingency tables', *Journal of American Statistical Association*, vol. 59 (1964b), pp. 319–52.

Goodman, L. A., 'Interactions in multidimensional contingency tables', *Annals of Mathematical Statistics*, vol. 35 (1964c), pp. 632–46.

Goodman, L. A., 'On the statistical analysis of mobility data', *American Journal of Sociology*, vol. 70 (1965a), pp. 564–85.

Goodman, L. A., 'On the multivariate analysis of three dichotomous variables', *American Journal of Sociology*, vol. 71 (1965b), pp. 290–301.

Goodman, L. A., 'The analysis of cross-classified data: independence, quasi-independence and interaction in contingency tables with or without missing cells', *Journal of American Statistical Association*, vol. 63 (1968), pp. 1091–1131.

Goodman, L. A., 'On partitioning chi-square and detecting partial association in three-way contingency tables', *Journal of Royal Statistical Society*, series B, vol. 31 (1969a), pp. 486–98.

Goodman, L. A., 'How to ransack social mobility tables and other kinds of cross-classification tables', *American Journal of Sociology*, vol. 75 (1969b), pp. 1–40.

Goodman, L. A., 'A modified multiple regression approach to the analysis of dichotomous variables', *American Sociological Review*, vol. 37 (1972a), pp. 28–46.

Goodman, L. A., 'A general model for the analysis of surveys', *American Journal of Sociology*, vol. 77 (1972b), pp. 1035–86.

Goodman, L. A., 'Causal analysis of data from panel studies and other kinds of surveys', *American Journal of Sociology*, vol. 78 (1973a), pp. 1135–91.

Goodman, L. A., 'The analysis of multidimensional contingency tables when some variables are posterior to others: a modified path analysis approach', *Biometrika*, vol. 60 (1973b), pp. 179–92.

Goodman, L. A., 'The relationship between modified and usual multiple-regression approaches to the analysis of dichotomous variables', in D. Heise (ed.), *Sociological Methodology, 1976* (San Francisco: Jossey-Bass, 1975).

Goodman, L. A., *Analysing Qualitative/Categorical Data: Log-Linear Analysis and Latent Structure Analysis* (Cambridge, Mass.: Abt, 1978).

Goodman, L. A., 'Multiplicative models for the analysis of occupational mobility tables and other kinds of cross-classification tables', *American Journal of Sociology*, vol. 84 (1979a), pp. 804–819.

Goodman, L. A., 'A brief guide to the causal analysis of data from surveys', *American Journal of Sociology*, vol. 84 (1979b), pp. 1078–85.

In this long series of papers, Goodman developed loglinear analysis until it became useful for social research. However, they are written for specialists and are not recommended for those without much mathematical confidence. Many of these papers are reprinted in Goodman (1978).

Goodman, L. A., and Kruskal, W. H., 'Measures of association for cross-classifications', *Journal of American Statistical Association*, vol. 49 (1954), pp. 732–64. Still the basic reference for measures of association. Many measures are described and compared.

Grizzle, J. E., Starmer, C. F., and Koch, G. G., 'Analysis of categorical data by linear models', *Biometrics*, vol. 25 (1969), pp. 489–504.

Haberman, S. J., 'Loglinear fit for contingency tables (Algorithm AS51)', *Applied Statistics*, vol. 21 (1972), pp. 218–25.

Haberman, S. J., *The Analysis of Frequency Data* (Chicago: University of Chicago Press, 1974). Haberman did much to develop iterative proportional scaling. Another text only for the statistically inclined.

Hauser, R. M., 'Some exploratory methods for modelling mobility tables and other cross-classified data', in K. F. Schuesslar (ed.), *Sociological Methodology, 1980* (San Francisco: Jossey-Bass, 1980), pp. 413–58.

Heise, D. R., *Causal Analysis* (New York: Wiley, 1975).

Hirschi, T., and Selvin, H. C., *Principles of Survey Analysis* (New York: Free Press, 1973).

Hornsby-Smith, M. P., and Lee, R. M., *Roman Catholic Opinion* (Guildford: University of Surrey, 1979).

ICPSR (Inter-Universities Consortium for Political and Social Research), National Data Program for the Social Sciences General Social Survey (Ann Arbor, Mich.: Institute for Social Research of the University of Michigan, 1972–8, annually).

Killion, R. A., and Zahn, D. A., 'A bibliography of contingency table literature: 1900–1974', *International Statistical Review*, vol. 44 (1976), pp. 71–112.

Knokke, D., 'A comparison of log-linear and regression models for systems of dichotomous variables', *Sociological Methods and Research*, vol. 3 (1975), pp. 416–33.

Lipset, S. M., Trow, M., and Coleman, J., *Union Democracy* (New York: Free Press, 1956).

Loether, H. J., and McTavish, D. G., *Descriptive Statistics for Sociologists* (Boston, Mass.: Allyn & Bacon, 1974).

Mack, J., 'Race and the Census', *New Society*, 27 July 1978, p. 191.

Merton, R. K., 'Contributions to the theory of reference group behaviour', in *Social Theory and Social Structure* (Glencoe, Ill.: Free Press, 1968), pp. 279–334.

Nelder, J. A., and Wedderburn, R. W. M., 'Generalised linear models', *Journal of Royal Statistical Society*, series A, vol. 135 (1972), pp. 370–84. Draws connections between loglinear analysis and other linear models, showing that they can all be fitted using iterative least-squares techniques.

Newport, F., 'The religious switcher in the United States', *American Sociological Review*, vol. 44 (1979), pp. 528–52.

Nie, N. H., Hull, C. H., Jenkins, J. G., Steinbrenner, K., and Bent, D. H., *Statistical Package for the Social Sciences*, 2nd edn (New York: McGraw-Hill, 1975).

Office of Population Censuses and Surveys (OPCS), *Classification of Occupations* (London: HMSO, 1970).

Office of Population Censuses and Surveys (OPCS), *The General Household Survey, 1973* (London: HMSO, 1976).

Office of Population Censuses and Surveys (OPCS), *The General Household Survey, 1974* (London: HMSO, 1977).

Office of Population Censuses and Surveys, *OPCS Monitor*, CEN 78/4 (London: OPCS, 1978).

Oppenheim, A. N., *Questionnaire Design and Attitude Measurement* (London: Heinemann, 1968).

Payne, C., 'The log-linear model for contingency tables', in C. A. O'Muircheartaigh and C. Payne (eds), *The Analysis of Survey Data*, vol. 2 (London: Wiley, 1977), pp. 105–44. A concise introduction which discusses the iterative least-squares as well as the iterative proportional scaling method of model fitting.

Plackett, R. L., *The Analysis of Categorical Data* (London: Griffin, 1974).

Reynolds, H. T., *The Analysis of Cross-Classifications* (New York: Free Press, 1977a). A good review of a number of topics relating to cross-classifications, including two chapters on loglinear analysis.

Reynolds, H. T., 'Some comments on the causal analysis of surveys with loglinear models', *American Journal of Sociology*, vol. 83 (1977b), pp. 127–43. A warning that the loglinear technique can yield misleading results, if not used with care.

Rosenberg, M., *The Logic of Survey Analysis* (New York: Basic Books, 1968). The definitive work on using elaboration to investigate multidimensional tables.

Runciman, W. G., *Relative Deprivation and Social Justice* (London: Routledge & Kegan Paul, 1966).

Stacey, M., Batstone, E., Bell, C., and Murcott, A., *Power, Persistence and Change* (London: Routledge & Kegan Paul, 1975).

Stouffer, S. A., Suchman, E. A., Devinney, L. C., Star, S. A., and Williams, R. M., Jr, *The American Soldier*, vol. 1 (Princeton, NJ: Princeton University Press, 1949).

Swafford, M., 'Three parametric techniques for contingency table analysis: a non-technical commentary', *American Sociological Review*, vol. 45 (1980), pp. 664–90.

Thornes, B., and Collard, J., *Who Divorces?* (London: Routledge & Kegan Paul, 1979).

Tukey, J. W., *Exploratory Data Analysis* (Reading, Mass.: Addison-Wesley, 1977).

Willer, D. E., *Scientific Sociology* (New Jersey: Prentice-Hall, 1967).

Zeisel, H., *Say it with Figures* (London: Routledge & Kegan Paul, 1958).

Index